SEX
FOR BEGINNERS

Writers and Readers

WRITERS AND READERS PUBLISHING, INCORPORATED
9 East 40 Street
New York, New York 10016

ISBN: 0–86316–011–5

1 2 3 4 5 6 7 8 9 0

Manufactured in the United States of America

About the Author and Illustrator

Errol Selkirk is a writer and editor living in New York City. He has been wild about sex since puberty. Only recently, however, has he been able to sublimate . Mr. Selkirk is also the author of *Computers for Beginners*.

Naomi Rosenblatt is currently the Art Director of Writers and Readers Inc. She did little illustration in this book and considers it a work of montage and survey, not a "hands on manual" unless you fashion it to become one. Naomi lives in a Manhattan apartment not much larger than this book.

Dedicated to

The continuing inspiration of Barry Shapiro
And
The living memory of Oscar Garcia

Images dedicated to my past demon lovers. I trust you
know who you are.

♡ Nomi

Introduction

"*Sex is not a mere physiological transaction . . . it implies love and love-making; it becomes the nucleus of such venerable institutions as marriage and family; it pervades art and it produces its spells and magic. It dominates in fact almost every aspect of culture.*"

—anthropologist Bronislaw Malinowski

From the beginning, sex was granted a special place in human affairs. The ancient Greeks compared the power of sexual attraction to the forces that coordinate the universe. Erotic feeling—like gravity and centrifugal force in today's physics—was believed to cause all things to come together, and all things to eventually fly apart.

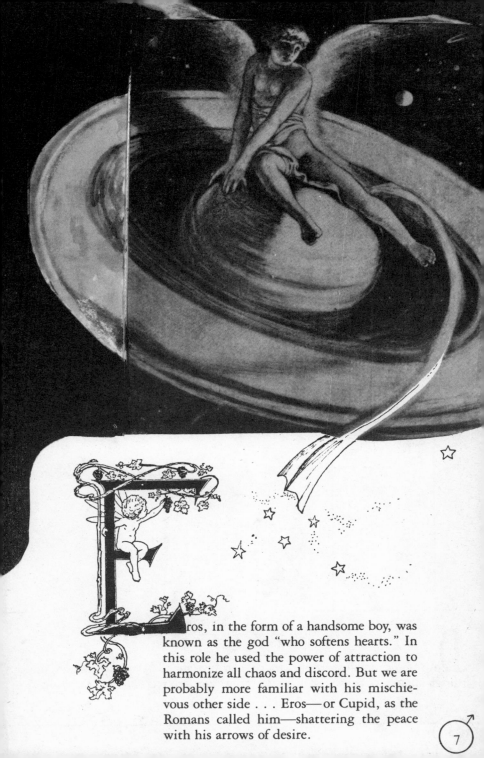

ros, in the form of a handsome boy, was known as the god "who softens hearts." In this role he used the power of attraction to harmonize all chaos and discord. But we are probably more familiar with his mischievous other side . . . Eros—or Cupid, as the Romans called him—shattering the peace with his arrows of desire.

Desire, and not just sexual desire, can be defined as a powerful response to things outside ourselves that we decide we need to feel satisfied.

Desire is what causes us to associate with other people. It encourages us to explore the possibilities of the world.

After all, if we need nothing, desire nothing—why bother getting up in the morning? Why bother producing food or shelter? Why bother getting to know other people or letting them get to know us?

We bother because we have to. People need each other. Humans are social animals . . . by desire.

Sigmund Freud, one of the first to create a philosophy of sex, believed that erotic attraction was the model for all other affectionate human relationships.

Desire is one of the paradoxes of human sexuality. Other mammals have a much easier time of it. They, like us, reproduce through sexual intercourse. But unlike people, they satisfy this need automatically through the physiological process of **estrus.**

Animals go into estrus—or heat—only when the female is sexually fertile. At other times, she is almost always uninterested in sex, or physically unable to perform it. But during estrus, everything is reversed: the female is interested in nothing else.

whew!

10

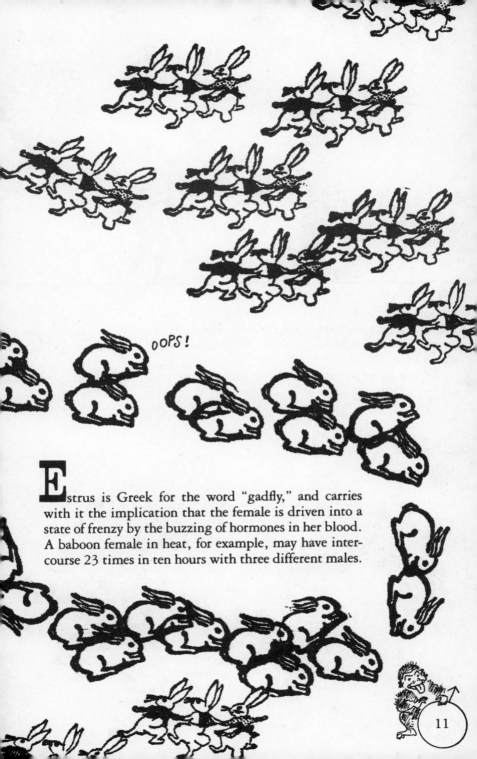

OOPS!

Estrus is Greek for the word "gadfly," and carries with it the implication that the female is driven into a state of frenzy by the buzzing of hormones in her blood. A baboon female in heat, for example, may have intercourse 23 times in ten hours with three different males.

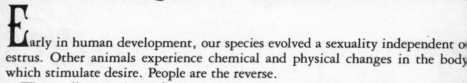

Early in human development, our species evolved a sexuality independent o estrus. Other animals experience chemical and physical changes in the body which stimulate desire. People are the reverse.

We usually experience desire through the eye and the mind first—and this produces changes in the body.

Freedom from estrus made human life possible.

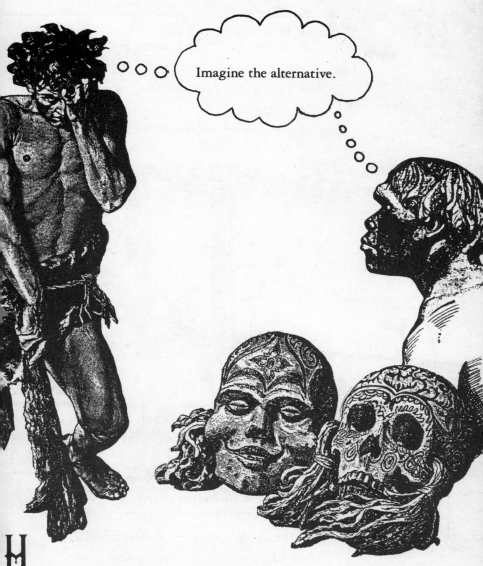

Imagine the alternative.

Human society functions because we—not a biological time clock—are capable of making **sexual choices.** We decide what we will do with our bodies . . .

This freedom is what makes our sex lives so rich and satisfying, as well as so complicated.

Sex means different things to different people:

To painter Andy Warhol, it is a subject that hardly deserves mention:

"Sex is the biggest nothing of all time."
—*painter Andy Warhol*

LOVE BOAT

To comedian Woody Allen it is an endless source of humor:

"I am a practicing heterosexual. But bisexuality immediately doubles your chances of a date on Saturday night."
—*comedian Woody Allen*

To psychologist Wilhelm Reich, sex is a serious matter relating to the health of the human organism.

"Psychic health depends upon orgasmic potency . . . upon the degree to which we can surrender to and experience the climax of excitation in the natural sex act."
—psychologist Wilhelm Reich

To feminist Kate Millet, sex is the basis for the unequal power balance between men and women:

"The situation between the sexes now, and throughout history, is . . . a relationship of dominance and subordinance."
—feminist Kate Millet

To critic Susan Sontag, sex can be viewed as a tool for self liberation: *"Sexuality—as something beyond good and evil, beyond love, beyond sanity; as a resource . . . for breaking through the limits of consciousness."*
—critic Susan Sontag

Others view sex as the basis of a chosen life style, as a fashion style,

or just another consumer product.

And still others see sex as a subject to be surveyed, or studied scientifically, or unraveled patiently, like a mystery, on the analyst's couch.

Even Freud confessed the difficulty of trying to pin down something as complex as sexuality:

"Seriously, it is not so easy to define what the term sexual includes."

The Sexes
"Everything connected with the difference between the two sexes is perhaps the only way of hitting the mark; but you will find that too general and indefinite."

Pleasure
"If you take the sexual act itself as the actual point, You will perhaps declare sexual to mean everything concerned with obtaining pleasurable gratification from the body."

Reproduction
If then you make the function of reproduction the kernel of sexuality you run the risk of excluding from it as a whole host things like masturbation or even kissing, which are not directed toward reproduction, but which are nevertheless undoubtedly sexual."

"Let us give up trying to do any better in this particular case."

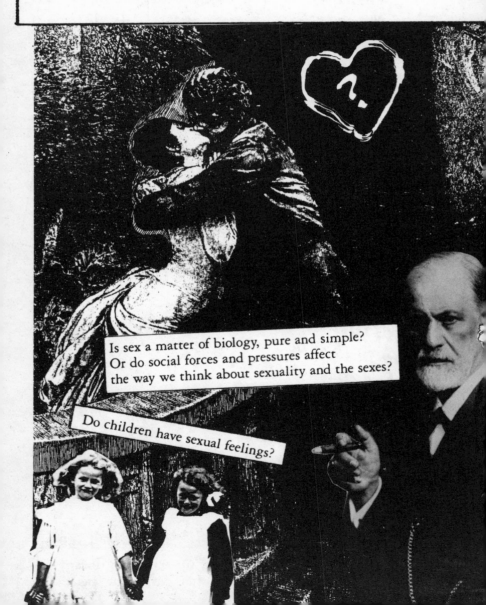

Today we are confronted by choices, bombarded by appeals to desire.
Making satisfying personal decisions about sexuality is not getting any easi
But even if we don't know all the answers, at least we can begin asking oursel
some of the important questions.

Is sex a matter of biology, pure and simple?
Or do social forces and pressures affect
the way we think about sexuality and the sexes?

Do children have sexual feelings?

What is normal sex? Why do some people naturally gravitate toward "unnatural" acts?
What is the connection between sex and power?
Is domination the ultimate aphrodisiac?
Why do some people associate sex and violence?

What do our sexual dreams and fantasies mean?

What is the connection between sex and love? Is romantic love a myth or a necessity? Do men and women have different ideas about love?

What can science tell us about the human sexual response?

How do religious ideas affect the way we think and feel about sex?

Why do ideas of sex appeal change over time and place?

Why is sex used so often in advertising?

Why are sexual relations in a culture so closely linked to social relations?

What can we learn about sex from art?

From language? From clothing and style?

What these questions show is that sex does not take place in a vacuum. Even when we're alone with another person in an intimate sexual situation, the room is filled with the feelings, fantasies, ideas and values we carry with us from the outside world.

Unless we understand some of the links between the world and our desires, how can we claim to have any sexual choices at all?

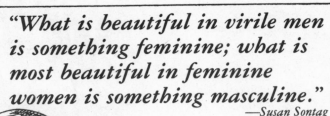

> *"What is beautiful in virile men is something feminine; what is most beautiful in feminine women is something masculine."*
> —*Susan Sontag*

Across the Great Divide

When we think of sex, we usually imagine the union of two people. But throughout history, sex has also been something that has divided us into groups:

The greatest division of all has been that between men and women. It has been used to set aside different social roles for both sexes, as well as different clothing, gestures, interests, occupations, expectations, and freedoms. Sex differences—real or imagined—have been used to create what feminist Kate Millet calls two "cultures": one male, the other female. What, if anything, do these separate cultures have in common?

The word sex comes from the Latin *secare*, meaning to section or divide. This concept of sex may be related to a myth popular throughout the ancient world about the creation of men and women.

Before there were humans there was Hermaphrodite, a peculiar creature with two faces, two sets of limbs, and one large body. The gods resented the fact that Hermaphrodite was so self-sufficient. In a jealous rage, they divided Hermaphrodite into two biologically interdependent sections: male and female.

Over the centuries, most societies have focused on the differences between the sexes, rather than the basic similarities. This emphasis has created a Big Myth about sex that persists in the world today.

According to this myth, men and women are opposites—with different kinds of intelligence, ability, feelings, and temperament. If one sex is active, the other must be passive; if one sex is rational, the other must be emotional; if one sex belongs out in the world, the other must belong back at home.

Is there any truth to this myth?

Biologically, the main difference between men and women is reproductive: men impregnate, women get pregnant, bear, and nurse children. Most other sexual distinctions result from this fact.

Physiologically, men and women produce different amounts of certain important hormones. Estrogen, a "female" hormone, governs the woman's reproductive system. It also has a role in breaking down nutrients and converting them to fat. Testosterone and other androgens are the "male" hormones. They have a role in building muscle in the man's body.

The androgens have often been linked to male aggression. Females and castrated males produce less androgen—and less aggressive behavior—than normal males. In one experiment with castrated mice, treatment with androgen produced a rise in aggression.

Does this mean that females are naturally less aggressive than males?

Yes

and no.

In another animal experiment with monkeys, females raised in the lab proved to be considerably more aggressive than those raised in nature. The lab animals lacked adult examples to learn from; essentially they did not have a monkey mother to show them the way they were supposed to act.

What causes the differences in male and female behavior? From the often contradictory evidence, sociologist Ann Oakley concludes:

"Biology may indicate the direction of the difference, although not its extent."

28

What this means is that another factor determines how great the differences between the sexes will be. And this is . . .

Society. Biology makes males and females. Society makes men and women. Masculinity and femininity are functions of gender—not sex.

Gender is the blueprint societies use to create their men and women.

society's ideas about gender are the source of most differences between men and women. Yet these ideas are often artificial and arbitrary. Ann Oakley explains:

"Every society uses biological sex as a criterion for . . . gender but, beyond that single starting point, no two cultures would agree completely in what distinguishes one gender from the other. Needless to say, every society believes that its own definitions correspond to the biological duality of sex."

50 50

There is nothing sacred, fixed, or universal about our ideas of masculinity and femininity. Here are some illuminating examples of sexual stereotypes from around the world:

Men in our society are supposed to be the sex–seekers. It's the masculine role to make a pass, initiate courtship, and always show an aggressive interest in having sex. But among the Zuni Indians of New Mexico, women are expected to make the first sexual move. Traditionally, the Zuni man faces the wedding night with fear and trembling. In the Trobriand Islands, the women also takes the lead. Anthropologist Bronislaw Malinowski reports that

"*On the whole, I think that in the rough usage of passion, the woman is more active.*"

31

Parenthood

Women in our society are supposed to have a powerful "maternal instinct" that automatically prepares them for parenthood. But among the Manus of the South Seas, only men are supposed to enjoy playing with children. Women in fact are revolted by the whole idea of being mothers.

In the Trobriand Islands the father is expected to share all aspects of child-raising. From the start, he cleans the baby and feeds it mashed vegetables; he fondles and carries it around. According to custom, only he will hold the child on his knee.

Along the same lines, the Australian aborigine father's role in parenting is considered so essential that a mother will put her newborn baby to death if the father dies during pregnancy.

Emotions

M en in our society are supposed to be able
to control their emotions, hide their feelings, and refuse to yield to sentiment or
pain. But in Iran, men are considered abnormal and untrustworthy unless they display
emotion, sensitivity and intuition. Iranian
men traditionally prefer poetry to logic.
Friends may touch each other and hold hands
in public—an intimacy that is considered
feminine in our culture. Women, in contrast, are expected to be the practical, cool,
and calculating sex.

Beauty

W omen in our society are supposed to make themselves attractive to men by adorning themselves with
cosmetics, perfume, jewelry, and revealing clothes. But
in Southwest Pacific societies, it is the men who wear
flowers and body scents. When young men are fully
costumed in all their festival finery, when they are made
up and perfumed, they are thought so irresistible that
they are not allowed to be left alone, for fear some
woman will seduce them.

33

Men in our society are supposed to be specially suited for the masculine role bread-winner and provider. Women are considered too weak and delicate physical labor; they are also thought too nonaggressive to be successful business. But in many African nations—such as Senegal, Gambia, and Kenya women customarily perform most of all the heavy farm labor. In this part of t world, when a man puts in a day's work, it is said he worked as "hard as woman."

Until recently women in our society were not expected to develop a career. T ideal in the West was that marriage and family *is* a career. But in Nigeria, woman is expected to learn a craft or trade. Among the Yoruba, a girl is n considered fit to marry unless she is able to earn a livelihood. As a result, tw thirds of the nation's trade is conducted and controlled by women. The examples should help to show that there is no one universal temperament males or females.

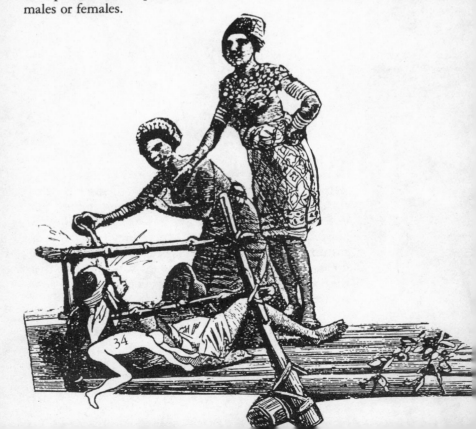

exual stereotypes about men and women may be myths or distortions—but
y are not illusions. Like self-fulfilling prophecies, they are powerful because
y are so widely accepted.

Feminist Kate Millet believes that these stereotypes are created and perpetu-
d in order to support our unequal social system. According to Millet, the
mation of human personality along rigid masculine or feminine patterns is
ed on

> *"the needs and values of the dominant*
> *group and dictated by what its members*
> *cherish in themselves and find convenient*
> *in their subordinates: aggression,*
> *intelligence, force, and efficacy in the*
> *male; passivity, ignorance, docility,*
> *'virtue,' and ineffectuality in the female."*

illet concludes that women under this system are prevented from developing
emselves beyond their biological function as wife and mother. As a result,
ery activity that can be described as distinctly human—rather than animal—
reserved for men.

In our society, children quickly learn who and what they're supposed to be. study of American four-year-olds showed that many or most could accurate distinguish the toys that were appropriate for both sexes.

The home is one of the first places where children learn the different social rol of men and women.

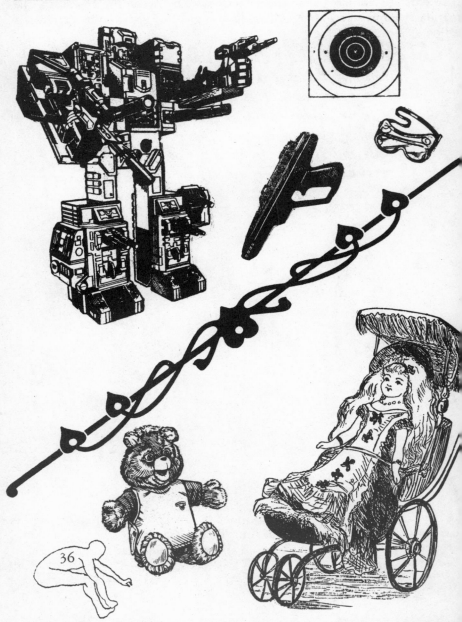

36

chool often reinforces this early lesson. For decades, sexual stereotypes filled most elementary textbooks. As late as the 1970's, a series of readers used by California school children contained 18 stories featuring the home. In twelve of them, the woman wears an apron and her chief occupations are shown as cooking, washing dishes, sewing, and ironing. The father's main occupation is coming home from work.

Textbooks for older students are often no better. When women are show working, their jobs are traditionally limited to typist, secretary, school teach waitress, and librarian. By default, men are shown doing every other kind work.

Ironically, girls perform better in school than boys at almost all grade leve Yet many girls suddenly stop achieving when they enter the teenage years. O possible reason for this decline is the hormone changes associated with puber But Ann Oakley offers another explanation:

"This is the time when each sex is being initiated into important aspects of its adult role. In the male role, achievement is stressed; in the female, conformity."

Further studies show that many teenage girls are afraid that continue achievement may result in a loss of femininity and popularity—viewed in term of competition with boys. Besides, high personal achievement is seen to be conflict with the traditional female career role of contented housewife.

Sexual stereotypes also take their toll on males growing up in our society. Many boys grow up in a home environment which encourages aggressive play and behavior. Emphasis on contact sports like football and hockey tends to institutionalize violence. And teenage boys often associate dangerous and anti-social acts with manly daring.

All of these factors contribute to the high crime and injury rate of male adolescents. In the mortality rate for 21 year-olds, 68% of the deaths are males. And later in life, men suffer twice as many heart attacks and strokes—aggravated by the stress involved in the need to achieve at any price.

Extremely macho men tend to view every area of human relations in terms of competition. Work, play, and sexuality are all viewed as opportunities for "scoring points." Or worse—as a form of warfare:

"Sex is not only a divine and beautiful activity: it's a murderous activity. People kill each other in bed."
—writer Norman Mailer

Men and women in our society begin their adult lives with a totally different orientation to the world and themselves.

Women's sense of self is usually based upon the ability to establish and maintain relationships with other people. Men base their sense of self on the ability to distinguish themselves in the world, usually through their work. Women sacrifice a firm sense of self for the experience of belonging; for men, the reverse is true.

If both sexes are allowed to develop, they move away from these absolutes as they mature. Men grow more interested in other people, and genuine love becomes possible. Women become more interested in developing a sense of self and personal achievement becomes necessary.

> "For men, intimacy becomes the critical experience that brings the self back into contact with others and makes it possible to see both sides—to discover the effects of actions on others as well as the cost of distance to the self. For men, intimacy brings an end to isolation."
>
> —psychologist Carol Gilligan

Women's self-evolution creates a need for a greater degree of independence and personal integrity. According to Gilligan, "This gives rise to the claim for equality, embodied in the concept of rights."

Growing up means giving up the old sexual stereotypes. So long as an individual believes it is more important to be a masculine man or a feminine woman—rather than a complete individual—he or she will remain an emotional adolescent, a fraction of a whole, a walking stereotype.

Let American revolutionary and feminist Emma Goldman have the last word on the topic:

"*A true conception of the relation of the sexes will not admit of conqueror and conquered; it knows of but one great thing: to give of one's self boundlessly, in order to find one's self richer, deeper, better.*"

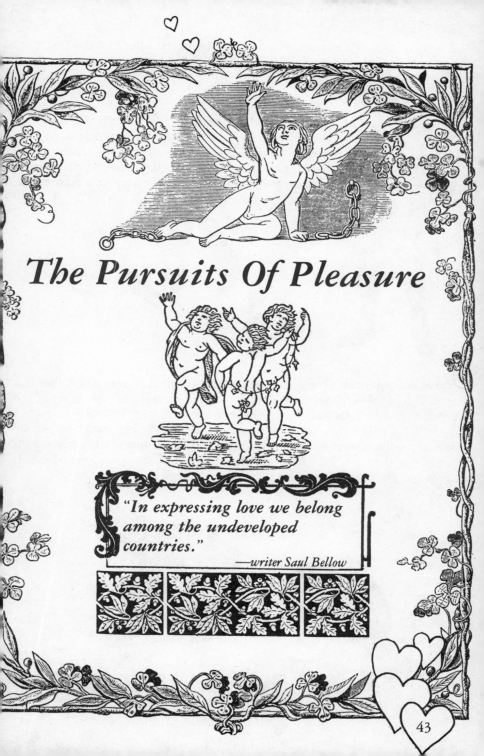

The Pursuits Of Pleasure

"In expressing love we belong among the undeveloped countries."

—writer Saul Bellow

The Christian missionaries who first arrived in the islands of the South Seas discovered that the natives didn't even know how to have sex properly.

Patiently the missionaries taught the islanders that the correct position was always with the man on top, the woman below. This posture reflected the male's natural superiority in the universe—and also kept sexual stimulation down the minimum necessary for reproduction.

Sexual attitudes often reveal a great deal about the structure and values of a society. The people of Samoa, for example, never appreciated the merits of the Missionary Position. In their culture men and women were more equal than in Europe. Why, under these circumstances, should the female always be below?

Besides, an islander might add, this position often hampers the woman with the weight of the man. Isn't it better that both parties stay active, so that each can give and get more pleasure?

After all, isn't that one of the main purposes of having sex?

That depends on where you are. Sexual relations are shaped by social relations. In cultures where men and women are viewed as opposites, there are usually two sexual codes.

This Double Standard reflects the balance of power between the sexes, expressed in terms of an individual's control over his or her own body.

In the Arab world, the balance of power is heavily tilted toward the male. A rich man can possess as many as four wives. Yet the Arabs also believe that women are naturally more highly-sexed than men. This conflict creates a number of social tensions.

Men fear that unless female sexuality is controlled, it could disrupt the whole structure of family and society they have created.

45

To this end, Arab women are strictly segregated. In some cases, even more severe methods are used, such as:

Clitorectomy so-called "female circumcision," in which part or all of a girl's sensitive clitoris is surgically removed.

and **Infibulation** in which the outer lips of the female organ are sewn or fastened together to prevent illicit intercourse.

Until recently, an estimated 90% of all Egyptian women were "circumcised" in this way in order to reduce sexual sensitivity. This practice was justified by one Sudanese source in these terms:

"Circumcision of women releases them from their bondage to sex, and enables them to fulfill their real destiny as mothers."

But sexual mutilation can also be psychological. In Victorian England, women were denied access to their sexuality in another way—through a nation-wide campaign of misinformation. Here's an example from Dr. William Acton, a prominent physician of the time:

"The majority of women (happily for society) are not very much troubled with sexual feeling of any kind. What men are habitually, women are only exceptionally . . . Love of home, of children, and of domestic duties are the only passion they feel."

The sexual ignorance that resulted from this campaign was so great that only one Englishwoman in four surveyed during this period knew she had a clitoris—or understood its role in producing pleasure.

Fear and guilt were also used where simple ignorance failed. For several generations, Victorian medicine—with the backing of government and church—continued to warn women of the high price they would pay for plea-sure. Influential doctors claimed that movement during intercourse could leave a woman childless, that sharp sexual stimulation could shorten lives, that female masturbation could cause insanity, and that oral sex could produce cancer of the mouth.

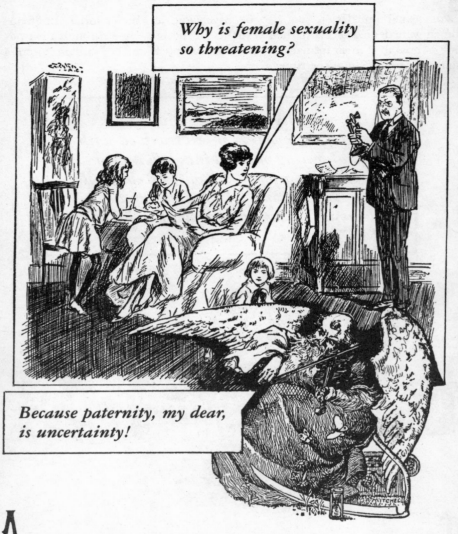

child will always carry the genes of its mother. It may, or may not, carry the genes of its mother's husband. How can a father ever really know that his children are his own?

Another reason is economics. In societies where women are financially dependent on men, where men control all available resources—a suspicious husband might wonder why he should invest his work and wealth in the children of another man's offspring. Why should he permit another man's children to inherit his possessions?

Uninhibited female sexuality undermines the foundation of the traditional father-dominated family on two fronts: biology and property.

An unfaithful wife threatens the paternity of all men. For this reason, she must be punished for her deed. And so long as men are free to engage in sex outside of marriage—with prostitutes, unmarried girls, and the wives of other men—there is no reason to encourage the sexuality of the women they marry.

The strength of the Double Standard grows out of this fusion of biology and economics. In cultures like the Trobriand Islands, where the link between sex and pregnancy was not completely understood until recently, there was only one single sex code for both men and women.

The Trobrianders were aware that virgins can't give birth. Intercourse is necessary to "open up" the woman, but the actual agent of conception is thought to be the spirit of an ancestor—not the father's sperm.

According to anthropologist Bronislaw Malinowski, who first studied the islanders in the early 1900's:

"Real kinship, that is identity of substance, 'same body,' exists only through the mother."

For this reason, wealth was passed down through the mother's line, a system called matrilinear succession. Matrilinearity is the custom in 15% of the world's cultures.

The Trobriand father was expected to "protect and cherish the children, to receive them in his arms when they are born," to be a teacher and a beloved friend. But he did not own them.

"The bearing of the wife toward her husband is not at all servile. She has her own possessions and her own sphere of influence, private and public."

Under these circumstances, there was no reason to try to control female sexuality. And since there was no "bride price" paid on the basis of a girl's virginity—females grew up as sexually free as males:

"At an early age children are initiated by each other, or sometimes by a slightly older companion, into the practices of sex . . . When speaking of these amusements the natives will frequently allude to them as 'copulation amusement,' or else it is said they are playing at marriage."

Another primitive society, the Tchambuli of New Guinea, recognize male paternity, but not male supremacy. Anthropologist Margaret Mead was surprised to learn what happens to the Double Standard when the roles are reversed.

Officially, Tchambuli culture is patrilinear; wealth is supposedly passed down to the children of the father. But in reality, the economic and sexual life of the people is dominated by the women, who fish, farm, and work together manufacturing trade goods.

Tchambuli women are self-assertive, practical, industrious, and cooperative, while the men are high-strung, wary of each other, and interested only in gossip and art.

The men constantly complain of hurt feelings, revealing what Mead calls "the pettishness of those who feel themselves weak and isolated."

Tchambuli men develop into skilled charmers. They wear lovely ornaments in their hair and flowers to attract the attention of the shaven-headed, unadorned women. Men are allowed to do the shopping, they carve beautiful objects in wood, paint, play the flute, and dance seductively for their female admirers.

"What the women think, what the women will say, what the women will do, lies at the back of each man's mind as he weaves his tenuous and uncertain web of unsubstantial relationships with other men. Each man stands alone . . ."

—Margaret Mead

The female's social dominance is clearly reflected in sexual relations. Young men are easily intimidated by their brides-to-be, and often refuse to sleep with them. Mead describes the typical Tchambuli man's situation:

"All that he hears of sex stresses the woman's right to the initiative."

Older men also fear that their wives will fall in love with the beauty of younger men. Widows, who are allowed to choose their own lovers, are considered especially passionate:

'No one expects her to remain quiet until her remarriage has been arranged. Has she not a vulva? they ask. This is the comment that is continually made in Tchambuli: Are women passive, sexless creatures?"

Animal studies confirm the connection between sex drive and social position. In one experiment, female rhesus monkeys were given the "male" hormone androgen—which is linked to sex drive in men and women. Those females who were dominant in the group before the experiment showed a marked increase in sexual activity. But those females with subordinate status had little or no reaction.

"Monkeys who physically dominate in a group sexually dominate the othe members," writes psychologist A.H. Maslow.

In human society, physical domination and status tend to be internalize within the individual. Social forces are transformed into attitudes and feeling

Maslow equates feelings of dominance with confidence, high self-esteem feeling of ability and usefulness, a high degree of independence, and a genera lack of shyness, timidity, embarrassment, and inferiority. Many psychologica studies have shown that dominant, self-confident women are most likely to b able to regularly experience orgasm and sexual desire.

These self-confident women are also less likely to accept a passive, strictly submissive role in sex. According to Maslow, these women get "a tremendous thrill out of occasionally assuming the 'above' position in the sex act; such behavior is unthinkable for women low in dominance feeling."

Submissive women, in contrast, are unable to assert themselves sexually. Satisfaction is totally dependent on the technical expertise of the male. Interviews show that these women are too embarrassed to tell their lovers what they want done to their own bodies. They complain that this would seem "selfish," "greedy," "animalistic," "unladylike," and "unfeminine."

The Double Standard, and the unequal power relationship it derives from and supports, is the worst possible basis for mutual sexual satisfaction. Lovers often must learn how to please each other and themselves. Yet men who are so aggressive that they are insensitive to their partner's needs—like women who are so passive that they can't express their desires—never get the opportunity to learn.

Ironically, human evolution has favored mutual gratification. Sexual pleasure made what was necessary for reproduction . . . enjoyable. And by helping to create emotional bonds between lovers, sex encouraged the development of family groupings.

57

Yet until Drs. William Masters and Virginia Johnson began their study of sexuality in the late 1950s, no one really understood how erotic pleasure was produced. Masters and Johnson used electronic and photographic observation, together with interviews, to discover that the human sexual response has four main stages.

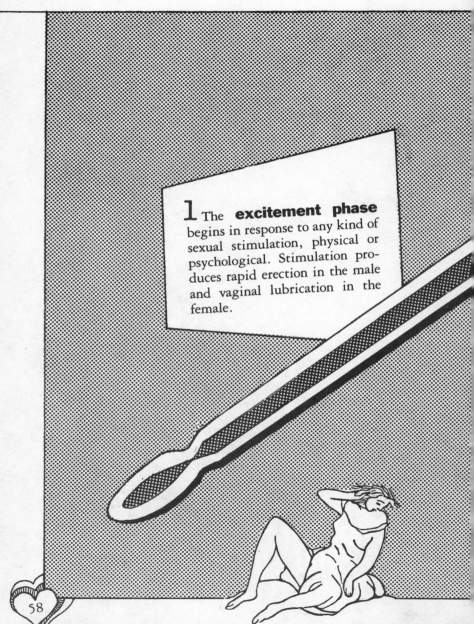

1 The **excitement phase** begins in response to any kind of sexual stimulation, physical or psychological. Stimulation produces rapid erection in the male and vaginal lubrication in the female.

3 In the **orgasmic phase**, orgasm proceeds with 8–10 powerful contractions in the sex organs. These contractions expel the fluids trapped in tissue and blood vessels—creating the pleasurable orgasmic sensations.

2 The **plateau phase** involves the intensification of sexual tension. Heartbeat increases; breathing becomes more rapid. The blood vessels of the pelvic area continue to swell.

In the female, the clitoris may now become erect. Continued stimulation will cause the clitoris to retract beneath the clitoral hood—a foreskin of flesh that normally surrounds it—a process that takes place 1½ to 2 minutes before orgasm. Retraction creates a small space below the clitoral hood. During intercourse, the clitoris is moved back and forth in the space by the thrusting of the penis in the vagina. This movement produces clitoral friction and higher levels of sexual tension.

4 In the **resolution phase**, following orgasm, the physiological signs of sexual tension dissipate.

Human sexuality has evolved in the direction of providing greater opportunities for pleasure. Early in the development of our species, we shed our covering of thick body hair in favor of smooth, sensitive skin. In effect, this turned our entire body into a unified erogenous zone.

Our sex organs are also positioned more frontally than other mammals, thus allowing us to have intercourse face-to-face— a substantial emotional refinement.

And humans, unlike our primate relatives the monkeys and apes, are able to experience sexual pleasure together. The importance of this capacity is explained by anthropologist Desmond Morris:

"The vast bulk of copulation in our species is obviously concerned not with producing offspring, but with cementing the pair-bond by providing mutual rewards for the sexual partners."

The pleasure bond between lovers must have had great importance to human evolution, according to biologist David Barash:

"Given that, during our evolutionary development, offspring were more likely to be successful if they received the committed assistance of at least two adults, selection would favor any mechanism that kept the adults together. Sex may be such a device . . ."

Emotional bonding through sex is not inevitable, but it certainly is common. Nowhere in the world is there a society where permanent sexual promiscuity is the rule. Some kind of more permanent relationship is always preferred.

Even in the uninhibited Trobriand Islands, Malinowski found that as children got older, sexual liaisons became more intense and longer lasting.

Sexual pleasure may indeed have helped to form the family. But is the monogamous family—one man, one woman—strong enough to contain the full force of sexual desire?

Is there a natural desire for sexual variety? Like everything else, there are at least two sides to this question. And not surprisingly, the battle lines have been drawn on the basis of sex.

The Men

Claude Lévi-Straus, noted linguist and anthropologist, takes the position that males seem to have a natural need for sexual variety:

"Even in a strictly monogamous society . . . this deep polygamous tendency, which exists among all men, always makes the number of available women seem insufficient."

The male's polygamous desire is part of our species' evolutionary heritage states biologist Donald Symons.

If all life forms seek to propagate their own genes—then the male has nothing to lose and everything to gain by having sex with as many females as possible.

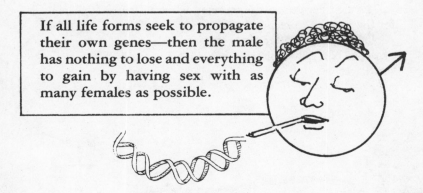

The female, in contrast, has little to gain from sexual variety—since she can only be made pregnant by one male at a time. And what the promiscuous female stands to lose is the loyalty and support of her mate.

Viewed in these terms, monogamy is a painful concession that men are force to make for women.

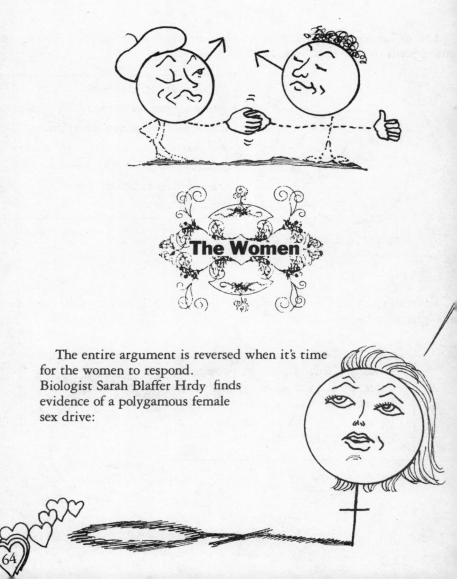

The Women

The entire argument is reversed when it's time for the women to respond. Biologist Sarah Blaffer Hrdy finds evidence of a polygamous female sex drive:

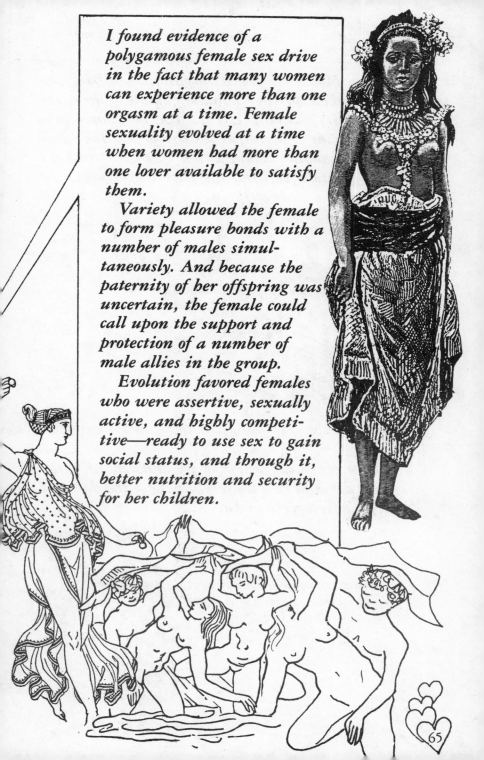

I found evidence of a polygamous female sex drive in the fact that many women can experience more than one orgasm at a time. Female sexuality evolved at a time when women had more than one lover available to satisfy them.

Variety allowed the female to form pleasure bonds with a number of males simultaneously. And because the paternity of her offspring was uncertain, the female could call upon the support and protection of a number of male allies in the group.

Evolution favored females who were assertive, sexually active, and highly competitive—ready to use sex to gain social status, and through it, better nutrition and security for her children.

65

Psychiatrist Mary Jane Sherfey carries the argument further:

> *Modern woman's orgasmic abilities are linked to the primate female's "insatiability" during estrus. The hormones producing a powerful sex drive "are the same hormonal combination which produces greatest fertility, the fewest abortions, the most viable offspring . . ."*

Yet the transition from ape to human created new social arrangement monogamy. Sherfey explains:

"The forceful suppression of woman's inordinate sexual demand was a prerequisite to the dawn of every modern civilization. . . ."

All things considered, monogamy is a painful sacrifice by both sexes, and for human society as a whole.

So, is there an ultimate purpose of sexual pleasure?

I'm glad you asked.

igmund Freud's philosophy of sex and society was based on the conflict ween the desire for pleasure and the demands of reality. Pleasure, for Freud, is result of gratifying the basic animal drives or instincts: when you're hungry, eat; when you're thirsty, you drink; when you're tired, you sleep; when 're angry, you strike; and when you are filled with erotic desire, you expel it ough sex. This is pleasure on the most elementary level.

Like children, early humans craved immediate gratification of all desires. F satisfaction as an end in itself has three serious drawbacks:

1. There is a limit to the amount of pleasure a person can absorb. If you eat or drink too much, for example, you will get sick or fall asleep. Too much of certain pleasures can be self-destructive.

2. There are also the demands of the environment to consider. Pleasure takes time and energy. If you're only busy enjoying yourself or sleeping it off—where will tomorrow's food and shelter come from? Will you be in a position to enjoy tomorrow's pleasures?

3. There are the desires of others to keep in mind. What you want may come into conflict with what other people around you want. If all you care about is your own pleasures—you may have to expend a lot of energy fighting off your angry neighbors.

There is the reality that early man had to face. As human communities beg to form, people painfully learned the value of putting aside or delaying imme ate satisfaction . . . in order to obtain longer-lasting benefits.

"Civilization is built upon the renunciation of instinctual gratification."

—*Sigmund Freud*

Instincts are never abolished, but the form they take can be modified, sublimated. The desire for inner gratification can be merged with the need to face the demands of outer reality. The endless quest for pleasure can be transformed into the pursuit of happiness.

In this way, the savage becomes human; the child becomes an adult.

reud believed that this developmental process was central to an understanding of sex. As societies and individuals evolve, the desire for constant, indiscriminate sex is replaced by an even more powerful urge. This is the desire to create deeper, more selective erotic bonds with certain people—based on trust and tenderness, as well as mutual attraction.

The desire for pleasure, in this its highest form, becomes that thing we know as

LOVE

you and your's
(paste photo)

The Erotic Wilderness

> "There is no more selfish passion than lust."
> —Marquis de Sade

Sexual desire has been compared to a

*powerful yearning,
a longing,*

a genital itch,

a consuming flame,

and madness doubled.

But these are all descriptions, not definitions. Exactly what is sexual desire?

Natural scientists try to explain
desire in physiological terms:

*Note its crucial role in reproduction and evolutionary
development. Isn't it just possible that desire is an affair of
the hormones?*

Social scientists argue that culture often
shapes sexual attitudes and practices:

*One society may believe that desire occurs automatically when
members of the opposite sex are in close proximity. Another
society may have no concept at all of spontaneous desire,
viewing sex as a sober process for making children. Isn't it
possible that social expectations are the real cause of desire?*

All of the sciences can yield important information about human sexuality, but none have actually been able
to explain desire as it is experienced.
For this kind of insight, what we need
is a philosopher: Jean Paul Sartre.

"*Desire is defined as trouble.*"
—Sartre

Trouble? As in troubled mind, troubled expression or look? Precisely. Trouble as when the normal flow of thoughts is disturbed by something. Sartre tries to show what he means with the example of troubled water. It remains water, but with something else added, something that disturbs its clarity and tranquility.

In the same way, desire is what happens when the mind is agitated or clogged by something else. But what? The body, of course.

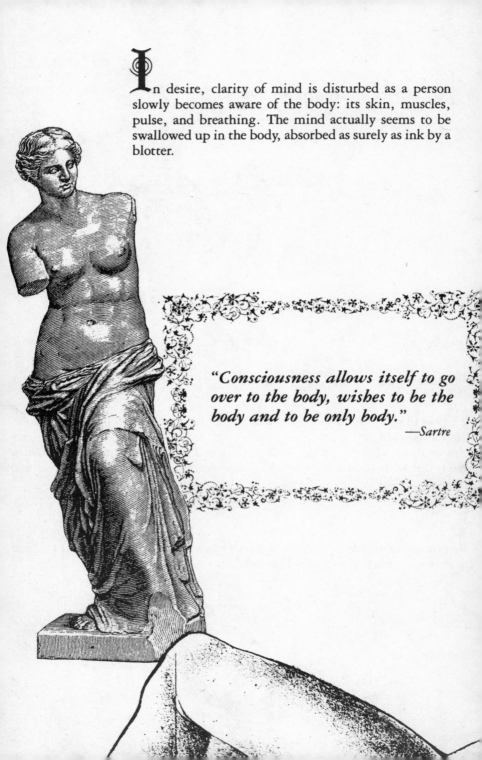

In desire, clarity of mind is disturbed as a person slowly becomes aware of the body: its skin, muscles, pulse, and breathing. The mind actually seems to be swallowed up in the body, absorbed as surely as ink by a blotter.

"Consciousness allows itself to go over to the body, wishes to be the body and to be only body."
—Sartre

This process begins voluntarily. We yield to desire. But once the decision has been made, the body seems to take over. The advanced signs of desire—faster pulse and breathing, increased sensitivity of skin and nipples, and erection of penis and clitoris—all occur automatically. These signs represent the further submerging of mind into the matter of the body.

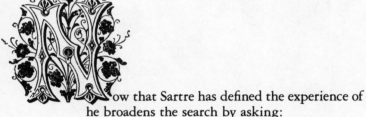

Now that Sartre has defined the experience of desire, he broadens the search by asking:

Desire for what?

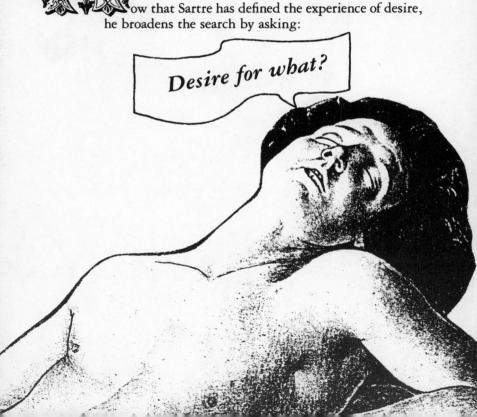

But the question now shifts to: Why desire a human being?

Because we are alone. Not only do we often feel cut off from other people—but we may also feel separated from the sense of our own body. Desire allows us to slip out of the hold of everyday consciousness. We stop thinking for a moment and start feeling. And as we begin to experience ourselves through the body, it also becomes possible to experience the world and other people directly . . . through feeling.

Sensations flood the mind. The eye suddenly seems to become an extension of the hand, capable of feeling the curves of another's body or sampling the texture of skin and hair.

The body, in turn, becomes crowded with consciousness—no longer just a machine for carrying around the brain. The surface of the skin is transformed into sensitive, feeling flesh.

It is the gentle touch of the caress that carries the transformation even further.

"The caress is not a simple stroking, it is a shaping. In caressing the Other I cause her flesh to be born beneath my caress, under my fingers . . . Desire is expressed by the caress as thought is by language."

—Sartre

The shiver of pleasure we feel when caressed this way is a sign of the awakening of our consciousness as flesh.

Desire is the attempt to make our body and the body of others exist as pure flesh. Flesh, in other words, for its own sake and for no other purpose: to handle and be handled, to press and be pressed against, to feel and be felt.

Sex, when seen in these terms, is a special way of being—existing sexually for someone who exists sexually for you.

But desire is not a matter of bodies alone. For other people to exist sexually for us, they must become flesh in their own eyes.

The final question is: Why is it so important to make love to the person *in* the body, as well as to the body itself?

> *"If the beloved is transformed
> into an automaton,
> the lover finds himself alone."*
> —*Sartre*

erpetual loneliness is the fate of those unwilling or unable to love. For some it
experienced as a vast emotional wasteland—a void of feeling. For others it is an
ferno of yearnings never to be satisfied. For all it is solitary confinement in a
vilight zone of the self that could be called . . .

The Erotic Wilderness.

One of the most outspoken voices in this wilderness is another French writer, Count Donatien Alphonse François de Sade, a man who preferred to be called:

The Marquis.

"Smitten stiff by desire, 'tis with yourself you must be solely concerned. And as for the object that serves you, it must always be considered as some sort of victim, destined to that passion's fury."

—Sade (1740–1814)

Who was Sade?
Why is just the mention of his name enough
to instill revulsion and stimulate curiosity at the same time?

Sade's name is forever linked to *sadism*—a sexual practice in which the pain of another person is used to increase one's own pleasure. In his personal life he is known to have abducted, tortured, and raped at least one woman, and to have poisoned with aphrodisiacs another three, all prostitutes. But these crimes alone would never have assured the Marquis his place in history.

Today, Sade is remembered as the author of a number of long pornographic works on philosophical themes. *Justine,* his most famous novel, is a rambling moral tale about the sexual humiliations and other misfortunes that befall a virtuous young woman in a thoroughly wicked world. In this novel, as in all of his writings, Sade's intent was to show the intimate connection between sex and power—a formula that ultimately equates coitus with cruelty.

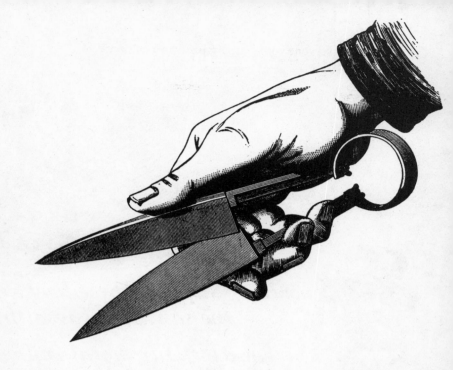

Power in all its forms was Sade's lifelong obsession. Throughout his works he depicted the unequal relationship between male and female, adult and child, the shrewd and the simple. But his special fascination was with social class— the institutionalization of unequal wealth and power.

Born in 1740, Sade grew up as a privileged person in a rigid class society. The France of that time was dominated by a tiny elite: the King, the rich nobles, and the Church hierarchy—mostly drawn from the ranks of the nobility. This dominant group made up less than 2% of the population—a mere 400,000 out of 25 million—but they owned most of the land and property.

Everyone could justify his own position:

KING:
"Divine Right!"

NOBLE: *"Superior breeding and the sanctity of wealth!*

CHURCH: *"Our moral influence over the people!"*

Everyone could justify his privileged portion. But when all the justifications were swept away, what remained was . . . *POWER.*

Power, even if it was arrogant and arbitrary—its possession, exercise, and enjoyment was no lie. For Sade, it became the most important thing in the world.

Imprisoned in the Bastille for his varied sex crimes and other indiscretions, Sade's fevered imagination went to work creating what writer Susan Sontag called a "negative utopia"—a worst-of-all-possible worlds, which nevertheless closely mirrored actual social conditions outside.

If an arbitrary class system divided humanity into warring groups of haves and have-nots, Sade created aristocrats who were ready to go the next step— and deny human status to the powerless.

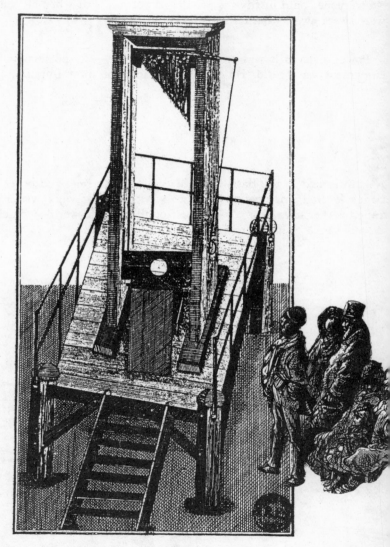

"Nature created human beings to no other end than that they amuse themselves on earth and make it their playground, its inhabitants their toys."

—Sade

If the powerful rich controlled the lives and labor of the poor, Sade fantasized situations which carried exploitation to its logical conclusions. In *Justine,* for example, a wealthy counterfeiter keeps female captives naked and enslaved in dungeon-like kennels, torturing and raping them as a sign of his mastery, and eventually working them to death chained to a wheel.

In Sade's next novel, *Juliette,* one of his monstrous autocrats goes even further. Not content to use the bodies of living women as holders for candles and serving tables for hot food—he actually eats their flesh and drinks their blood, a practice writer Angela Carter called "the most elementary act of exploitation."

Sade presents a world stripped to its brutal basics: Power is the only relationship between people that matters. Pain and pleasure are the only pure emotions uncontaminated by wishful thinking and superstition. Good and evil are issues that can be reduced to sensations—how much, how little. Strictly scientific questions.

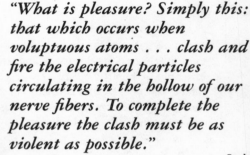

"What is pleasure? Simply this: that which occurs when voluptuous atoms . . . clash and fire the electrical particles circulating in the hollow of our nerve fibers. To complete the pleasure the clash must be as violent as possible."

—Sade

ade's characters are not only alienated from each other, they are also out of touch with their own bodies. When unable to feel pleasure anymore, they order themselves whipped. No sacrifice is too great to feel *something*.

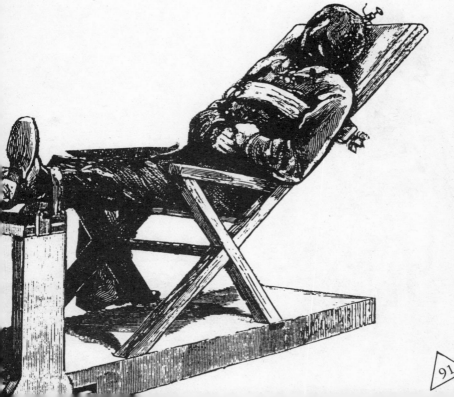

Even at an orgy, individuals remained locked in themselves, untouched, uninvolved. In Sade's theatre of cruelty, there is no room for improvization. Sex is mechanical, well-rehearsed and choreographed, perversely restrained. Intimacy is replaced by spectacle.

Instead of lovers, Sade presents us with masters and slaves. Instead of mutu gratification, the best he can offer is satisfaction in sequence.

Pleasure as a feeling is not the theme of Sade's work. But pleasure—especially the forbidden pleasure of transgression—is valued as an *idea*.

"Beauty, virtue, innocence . . . these qualities also afford us the opportunity of violating another prohibition; I mean, offer us the kind of pleasure we get from sacrilege . . ."

—*Sade*

For Sade, the triumph takes place in the mind. Sex is something that is done for the sake of mastery—not for its own sake. And since the Sadean refuses to release conscious control long enough to become flesh, he or she cannot use the flesh of another except as a symbol of submission. The result is that he or she is just as alone as before.

rgasm, extracted only after great exertion, yields only slight relief. True, the elf is silenced for a moment by sexual climax—what the French call "the little leath." But the longings soon return with a vengeance.

Desire of the flesh can be gratified in the flesh. Desire as an idea knows no limits.

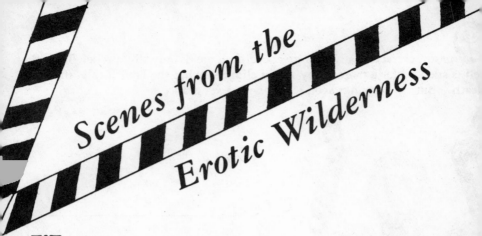

Scenes from the Erotic Wilderness

Welcome to a world in which sexual desire is almost exclusively enjoyed as a idea.

Thirty years ago, when Eldridge Cleaver was a young man, long before h became a revolutionary Black Panther, he deliberately used sexual assault as a too in the service of an idea. Like Sade, his aim was transgression.

"Rape was an insurrectionary act. It delighted me that I wa defying and trampling on the white man's law, upon his system of values, and that I was defiling his women."

—*Eldridge Cleav*

leaver justified rape as a fit response to America's long history of slavery and
ite supremacy.

'or these real and horrible crimes, he wanted justice, and he proudly saw
nself assume the role of the racial avenger. But his hidden feelings toward sex
women—all women—were betrayed by another confession:

"To refine my technique and modus operandi, *I started practicing on black girls in the ghetto."*
—*Eldridge Cleaver*

The average rapist is no weirdo, no psychotic or schizophrenic beset by timidity, sexual deprivation, and a domineering wife or mother. That's the myth. According to an FBI report quoted by writer Susan Brownmiller, "The typical American perpetrator of forcible rape is little more than an aggressive, hostile youth who chooses to do violence to women."

Rape is the no-frills sadism of this group. Exaggerated pride of self—a trait they share with Sade—is closely linked with sexual aggression and violence. This is the mentality of *machismo*, which means "maleness" in Spanish. But its effects can be seen wherever young men feel the need to assert their physical power against the defenseless.

Contrary to popular belief, the majority of rapes are not the spontaneous explosions of individuals with pent-up emotions and uncontrollable lusts. According to a nationwide study by sociologist Menachem Amir, most assaults are premeditated. Many are group efforts—brutal "gang bangs." Almost all involve some kind of violence, show of weapons, or even threats of death.

This pattern follows for prison rapes against vulnerable male inmates, as well as the estimated 250,000 sexual assaults that take place against women in the streets and homes of America.

For older, wealthier, more respectable men, sexual power is usually not wielded through physical force. Authority—in the form of sexual harrassment on the job—and the irresistible lure of money assert mastery with far less personal risk.

In prostitution, like any of Sade's negative utopias, it is generally the weak who cater to the sexual demands of the strong.

True, there are exceptions. But the mass of street-walkers, male hustlers, and massage parlor workers is composed of the young, the poor, the unskilled, and often the addicted. The powerless, in other words.

Regardless of the situation, the prostitute offers the patron pre-scripted, tailor-made sexual performance. Sex—packaged like any other wonderworking consumer product. Reporter Gail Sheehy, in a series of investigative articles, reveals the secret appeal of the prostitute.

paid girl . . . relinquishes all rights to make emotional or sexual demands. She would never call his office the next morning and leave an embarrassing message. It is her stock in trade to encourage men's sexual fantasies and exploit them. The man who is less than certain of his 'sensuousness' knows he will be safe in his old habits. It is the prostitute's job to recreate, if only for ten minutes, the ancient rite of dominance/submission that can induce sexual competency."

Others in the Erotic Wilderness are so attached to sexual symbolism that they can dispense with a human partner altogether. A prime example is the *fetishist* who is attracted to objects associated with a sexual partner, rather than to a flesh and blood person. Gay writer Jean Genet describes the power of the fetish in this encounter with a policeman:

> *"I was excited chiefly by the irresistible presence of his inspector's badge. That metal object had for me the power of a cigarette lighter in the fingers of a workman, of the buckle of an army belt, of a switchblade . . . objects in which the quality of maleness is violently concentrated."*

To one degree or another, most of us are at least latently fetishistic. We are partial towards certain things about other people—appearance, dress, voice quality and accent, even physical odor.

The difference is that our interest leads us into relations with these people. The fetishist, on the other hand, pursues sexual objects as a substitute for human relations. Solitary masturbation, not sexual contact, is the goal of the true fetishist.

What causes fetishism? Nobody really knows for certain. Individual cases differ, but most psychologists view it as an erotic throwback to the attachments of childhood.

CHOOSE
YOUR
FAVORITE:

Voyeurism is another flight from human contact. Like fetishism, it is a form of sexuality in which erotic possibilities are severely limited. Here the main excitement comes from viewing the bodies of others—on display or engaged in sexual acts.

For most of us, a view of the naked body can also often be a stimulus to desire. But for the voyeur, the main outcome of desire is masturbation. He or she will generally have no interest in—or even feel revulsion towards—actual sexual contact. All that is interesting is the potent symbolism of the naked body.

Pornography is another form of voyeurism, one in which the photograph or printed storyline has completely removed the need for human contact.

107

The unclothed body is the original fetish object. Flesh is truly an invitation to desire. But a pornographic picture is only the illusion of flesh: an assembly of dots on a piece of paper. It may have the power to arouse desire, but it cannot satisfy it.

Feminists like Angela Carter oppose pornography for this reason:

"Pornography involves an abstraction of human intercourse in which the self is reduced to the probe and the fringed hole, the twin signs of male and female in graffiti, symbols scrawled on the subway poster and the urinal wall, the simplest expression of stark and ineradicable sexual differentiation, a universal language of lust."

Carter points out that her anatomy is only one part of an infinitely complex organization—herself. Pornography strips away what makes each person unique and human, and focuses only upon our sexual existence as mammals.

Pornographic pictures, of course, are not simple portraits. Unlike photos of naked people appearing in art or medical texts, porn is intended to do more than accurately depict the body and its parts. Porn's function is to produce sexual excitement.

Pornography is not reality—with the sexy parts thrown in for good measure. Porno tells us only what we expect to hear. It doesn't slow down the action by presenting real people having real sex. It achieves its mission through the simpler, much more direct route of manipulating sexual symbols.

The most basic symbols, naturally, are images of the sex organs and other erotically-charged parts of the body. But these areas get their power to excite from the context in which they appear.

The situation of the model is key to the meaning and erotic impact of the picture. Porno, after all, is posed.

Even when the situation seems innocuous—for example, a Playboy centerfold emerging from a bath—the viewer knows that the situation was staged for his pleasure. It isn't a snapshot; it didn't just happen. For some viewers, the posed picture is an attraction in and of itself.

There is also potent symbolism in the kind of posing found in pornography. The model is often shown reclining on a couch or bed, clearly on display. He or she is also often portrayed thrusting out parts of the body to the viewer, as if asking to be sampled like a ripe fruit.

A second popular pose shows the model with arms crossed over the head—al but tied at the wrists. Sometimes he or she will be portrayed clasping the barred headboard of a bed, as if simulating the role of the handcuffed prisoner.

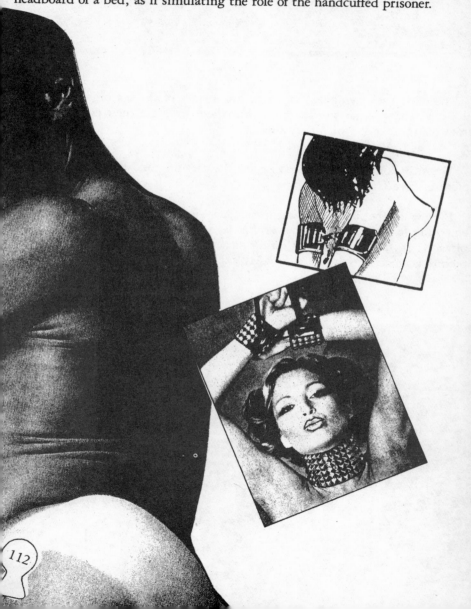

Another common pose depicts the model from the rear on all fours, buttocks raised, legs spread, and head turned around to face the viewer. This, as any zoologist will testify, is the visual sign one ape gives another as an invitation to sex. The position is called "presenting," and it also happens to be the way one animal signifies its submission—physical and sexual—to another.

Finally, there is the symbolism of the eyes, the message of the inviting glance. Here, however, we see only a simulation of desire. The model is supposed to seem as if she's aroused and welcomes our attentions. But like the prostitute, the model only appears to want IT—not because she or he wants it—but because *you* want IT.

Pornography, in fact, is paper prostitution.

113

The mystique of the whore and hustler attract many of us. But we also may hate and fear them for their ability to exploit our desire. In homosexual porn, the reader is often expected to identify with the tough hustler who treats the hapless *john* with all the cruelty he needs and deserves. Here the hatred is turned back upon itself—and partly upon the reader.

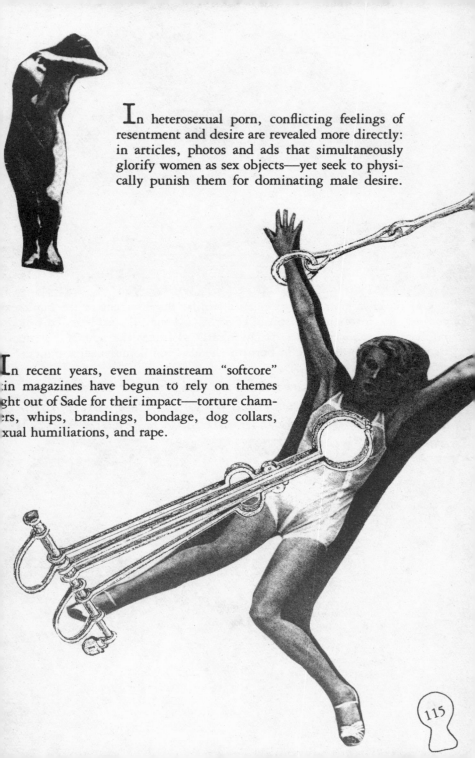

In heterosexual porn, conflicting feelings of resentment and desire are revealed more directly: in articles, photos and ads that simultaneously glorify women as sex objects—yet seek to physically punish them for dominating male desire.

In recent years, even mainstream "softcore" kin magazines have begun to rely on themes ght out of Sade for their impact—torture chambers, whips, brandings, bondage, dog collars, xual humiliations, and rape.

Gay novelist John Rechy reports a similar development in the homosexual community, involving the spread of S&M (sadomasochism) bars, bath house publications, and costumes. Rechy clearly identifies the powerful symbolism that occupies center stage in both the hetero- and homosexual variants of the erotic theatre:

"Black is the dominant color . . . in effect, a costume of death—an effect corroborated by an article on necrophilia in an S&M magazine: As if the ultimate celebration of S&M were death."

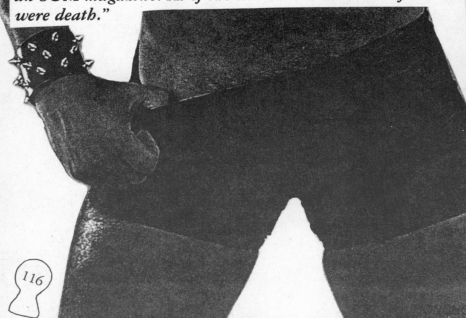

Even when physical death or injury does not occur, another sort of death, a spiritual extinction, is inevitable.

> *"Stiff, posturing clients in leather bars often resemble mannequins manufactured with various degrees of attention from one iron mold . . . The appeal of the costume is such that some gay men will only go with another in full regalia, in effect to make it with the costume."*

Sadomasochism is the spectacle of individuals surrendering themselves to the symbolism of power. In this theatre of cruelty, the theme of the drama is domination and submission. Sex is often only a pretext, a vehicle for acting out conflicts and fantasies about the individual's relationships to others. Sex is almost incidental.

The Erotic Wilderness in all its forms is a betrayal of Eros. It is the living body of sex stripped to a skeleton of symbols, the flesh reduced to the image, the spontaneous caress to the scripted gesture and response, and possibilities of love to the calculations of solitude.

ere we learn the price of banishment from our own species, the certain death
body and spirit that follows when Eros is denied its true function of bringing
together.

The Party of Eros

"*The sexual question must be politicized.*"
—*Wilhelm Reich*

120

In 1872, Victoria Woodhull became the first woman to run for President of the United States. Her program called for taxes on the profits of the rich, free courts of justice for the poor, an end to the death penalty, world government, and naturally, women's right to vote. As radical as these proposals seemed at the time, what really scandalized America were Woodhull's social demands: birth control, easier divorce, and *free love.*

"Yes, I am a free lover! I have an inalienable, constitutional, and natural right to love whom I may, to love as long or short a period as I can, to change that love every day if I please."

For centuries, the call for "free love" or what we today might call sexual liberation has been a key part of nearly every radical program for political change. Reformers and revolutionaries alike have linked oppressive social systems with repressive, uptight sexuality—and have opposed them both.

121

Yet is there really a direct connection between the values and institutions of people and their sexual practices? Judging from history, the answer is a resounding YES!

you bet!

ROME was a world empire based upon military conquest. It shouldn't come as a surprise that one of this society's most influential writers, Ovid, would write a book called the *Art of Love* that compared sexual seduction to the siege and sack of a city.

Sex and violence merged in Rome's gladiatoral games, where prostitutes waited under the arches of the Coliseum to serve those whose passions had been inflamed by the sight of other men's blood. The word fornication, in fact, comes from the Latin for archway—*fornix*.

I SAW...I CONQUERED...I CAME

GREECE had as its highest ideal excellence, and the honor that came from achieving or possessing it. Gentlemen of means, with property and slaves, had ample leisure to develop mind and body. Unfortunately, while not having to work for a living made the excellence of the few possible—it also made the domination of the many necessary. And Greek sexuality clearly reflected that fact.

Women as a class were heavily oppressed. They were segregated in the woman's quarter of the home, veiled and chaperoned in the street, given no more education than they needed to cook or sew, prohibited from inheriting money, and allowed no right to divorce. Sexually—and in every other way—woman's role was to serve.

"We have courtesans for the sake of pleasure, prostitutes for the daily health of our bodies, and wives to bear us lawful offspring and be the faithful guardians of our homes."
—*Demosthenes*

"Is there anyone with whom you talk less than you do with your wife?"
—*Socrates*

For love, Greek gentlemen often turned to the handsome youths exercising naked in the gymnasium. Yet even this love between males was no affair between equals. In its idealized form, the youth exchanged his favors for what the man could teach about being a gentleman: self-defense, how to speak and think intelligently, a love of poetry, wine, and the finer things of life.

Yet in its erotic reality, Greek homosexuality distinguished between the active lover and the passive love object—the beloved youth. For this reason, it was thought inappropriate for the youth to experience sexual pleasure in the love embrace. According to the logic of domination, this alone was the right of the man.

CHINA, from the earliest days, based its society on principles of change and balance derived from close observation of nature and farming. This tradition culminated in the wisdom of the Tao—or the Way—as set down by the great Chinese visionary Lao Tzu. For Taoists, sex was an exchange of energy that led to health and long life. To give pleasure to a lover was thought to increase the benefit for both parties.

Even today, the Taoist division of the universe into the ever-changing qualities of Yin and Yang—female and male, earth and sky, dark and light—is central to Oriental philosophy. We can still see Lao Tzu's influence in Zen Buddhism, Japanese macrobiotics, Chinese medicine, acupuncture, and even the writings of Mao Tse Tung.

But under the later influence of Confucius, conservative social values began to dominate China. Sexual emphasis shifted to the duty of producing many heirs. The role of women was diminished as the rich rushed to amass harems. And because of increased sexual demands made upon the man, erotic prudery became necessary in everyday life—in order to limit the temptation to expend sperm for any other purpose than reproduction.

JAPAN had its own unique attitude toward sex. Although women held a lowly position in society, the highest class of prostitutes—known as Geishas—were admired for their talent, refinement, and beauty in what was known as "The Floating World." Here women possessed a status unattainable in the outside world. And it was here that the Geishas inspired the creation of kabuki theatre, Japanese music and poetry, and the famous erotic woodcuts known as Ukiyo-E. All of these artistic expressions were tinged with a sensuality that glorified the ephemeral delights of life in The Floating World.

127

INDIA had two conflicting cultural ideals for its upper classes: the mystic and the merchant. Tantric sex was developed as a mystical tool for spiritual power and enlightenment. The main technique involved learning how to experience orgasm without ejaculation. This was believed to strengthen the spirit. Union of male and female sides of the self was viewed as the basis for inner peace. This idea is mirrored in Hindu religious art and in the important mantra or prayer: *OM MANI PADME OM.* It means the jewel is in the lotus, the male is in the female

Sex for a member of India's relatively large and prosperous middle class was more a matter of family business and personal pleasure. Merchants were advised to dress each marriageable daughter smartly and send her "where she can easily be seen by all . . . to show her advantage in society, because she is a kind of merchandise." Young men of this class had the money and leisure to practice the sexual sophistications of the Kama Sutra with paid courtesans.

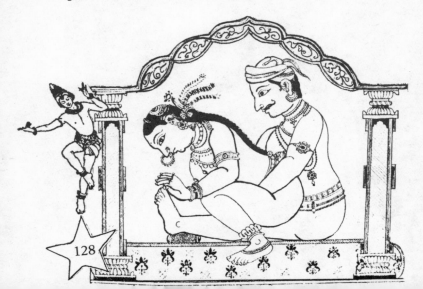

128

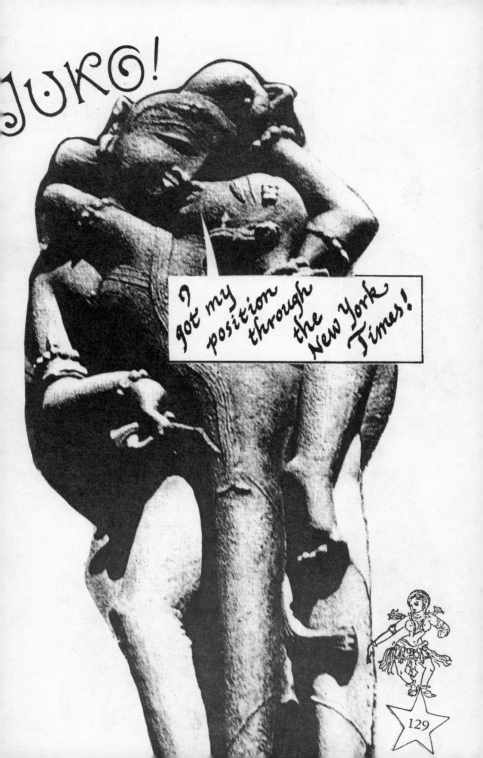

Our own sexual heritage in the West
still bears the scars of another kind of conflict:
The conflict between the body and the soul. Christian
doctrine from the earliest days rejected the physical
pleasures of this world for the spiritual rewards of the
world to come. Total celibacy was preferred by the early
Church. But in the words of the apostle Paul:

"Better to marry than to burn."

What about children then? For most early Chris-
tians, kids were just so much unnecessary baggage.
Any day Jesus would return. The faithful would then be
blessed with immortality in the Kingdom of Heaven.
Under those circumstances, what use was the precarious
immortality of parenthood?

Over centuries, the Church adjusted to the idea that Christ might not return a while. In order that the congregation might survive, sex within marriage the express purpose of reproduction became more acceptable.

But the underlying Christian hostility to sex and the human body can still be een in this statement by Church theologian, Tertullian, who actually castrated imself in the service of his beliefs two centuries after Paul:

"Marriage and fornication are different only because the laws appear to make them so; they are not intrinsically different, but only in the degree of illegitimacy. For what is it that all men and women do in both marriage and fornication? They have sexual intercourse, of course."

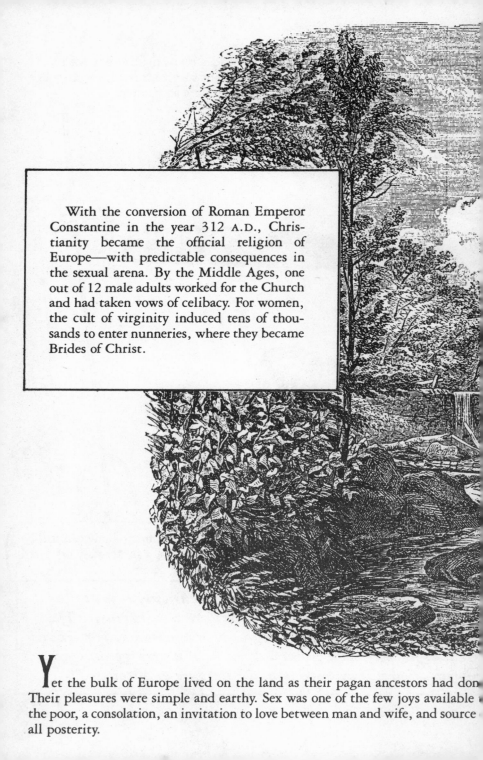

With the conversion of Roman Emperor Constantine in the year 312 A.D., Christianity became the official religion of Europe—with predictable consequences in the sexual arena. By the Middle Ages, one out of 12 male adults worked for the Church and had taken vows of celibacy. For women, the cult of virginity induced tens of thousands to enter nunneries, where they became Brides of Christ.

Yet the bulk of Europe lived on the land as their pagan ancestors had done. Their pleasures were simple and earthy. Sex was one of the few joys available to the poor, a consolation, an invitation to love between man and wife, and source of all posterity.

Sex had also long been linked to the mysteries of fertility—to planting and to harvest—and it was only natural to want to coax a little extra production out of the ground by dedicating a field to nature or to God, and then making love on it.

So the Church had its work cut out for it.

Speeches, sermons, cathedral statues, stained glass windows, paintings, a volume after volume of legal and religious punishments were created solely discourage everything from masturbation and oral sex to adultery and pries marriage.

The sex drive of an entire continent was relentlessly driven undergrou perverted into such sadomasochistic practices as flagellation and torture.

Church hyposcrisy was notorious. In England, the Bishop of Winchester actually chartered and controlled the houses of prostitution used by his London congregation. Abbots had to be warned against sleeping with the younger monks in their charge. Priests seduced parishioners right behind the altar. Bishops used nunneries like harems. And several Popes created entire dynasties of illegitimate children. Yet few dared to openly question the Church's official antagonism to the sex drive it tried so hard to control.

Martin Luther (1453–1546), leader of the Protestant Reformation, attacked the official Catholic position on the superiority of virginity over marriage.

He claimed that the whole notion of God's special love for virgins was t product of deviltry, and its effect was to corrupt the clergy. Accordingly, Prote tants closed monasteries and nunneries, and allowed their ministers to marry. Y that didn't mean that Luther was able to escape Christianity's ancient hostili to sex:

> *"Intercouse is never without sin; but God excuses it by His grace, because the estate of marriage is His work."*
>
> —*Luther*

Other Europeans soon began to question the traditional link between sin and sex. One group, called the Brothers and Sisters of the Free Spirit, based their free sexuality on the relationship of Adam and Eve—before the legendary Fall from Grace. Known as Adamites, they worshipped naked in secret congregations called Paradise. Group sex was practiced as a celebration of shared love.

Dutch painter Hieronymous Bosch (1450–1516), the sect's most famous member, may have used Adamite meetings as the model for some of his fantastical paintings.

The Brothers and Sisters were eventually exterminated by the Inquisition. But the idea that people could live in peace with each other and with their own sexual natures continued to influence Western thought.

For the next two centuries, European thinkers proposed various Utopian schemes for human social and sexual liberation. In the mid 1700s, philosopher Jean-Jacques Rousseau concluded that man in his natural state was a Noble Savage—much like the strong, healthy Indians of North America and the natives of Polynesia. Rousseau insisted that man's troubles came not from his own evil nature, but from the malformation of so-called "civilization," itself crippled by institutionalized greed, religious superstition, and tradition.

The coming of the French Revolution in 1789 provided the first real chance to transform mankind by reshaping the institutions and values of society. A first step was adopting a Declaration of the Rights of Man. This was passed. But when female revolutionaries tried to present a Declaration of the Rights of Women, they were hooted out of the Assembly.

Bonaparte's rise to power effectively ended the Revolution. Women's rights were actually rolled back and frozen in the Code Napolèôn, which made all females permanent wards of their fathers, husbands, and brothers. For women, at least, the Revolution hardly happened at all.

"Is that all there is?"

137

Another kind of revolutionary change was taking place at the same time in England. The centers of power and the sleepy little farm towns were both being transformed by . . .

Industrialization, the influence of the old land-rich aristocrats was being replaced by the money and power of a new, capitalist ruling group made up of industrialists, financiers, merchants, and professionals. The New Rich were terrified by the recent upheavals in France. And they blamed all the trouble on the lax morals of the pleasure-seeking French aristocracy, who were simply too decadent to fight or change.

Accordingly, The New Rich endorsed a system of sexual values firmly based upon the Protestant Ethic: deferring immediate gratification for long-term gain.

The factory and the banking house became the models for a peculiar view of sex that was linked to the social values of production and accumulation—making money and saving it up.

Human sexuality was viewed as a closed system. Each man's lifetime production of sperm was considered to be fixed and limited. To "expend" or "squander" one's reproductive assets on mere pleasure was thought to be more than a bad biological investment. It was crazy. And it supposedly led to eventual madness and death.

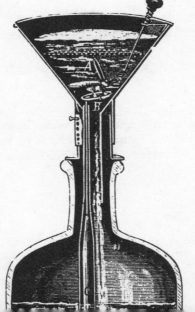

Prudery. Ignorance. And Hypocrisy.

Welcome to the long reign of Queen Victoria. Under the dominant values of production and accumulation, temptations had to be kept to a bare minimum. Victorian doctors warned that sex more than once a month could seriously injure the nervous system.

140

Only 100 years ago, volumes were published by some of England and America's greatest medical specialists describing the dire effects of a wholly illusionary disease called *spermatorhea,* caused by habitual dissipation of sperm. To prevent wet dreams, some unfortunate children had their hands bound nightly in bed. Others actually had diabolical devices attached to their genitals.

Adults tried to avoid stimulation by pretending to ignore the fact that they too had bodies.

141

The human form was supposed to be totally clothed from head to foot. Sensible people were advised to cover themselves in the bathrub, so as not to unduly excite themselves with a glimpse of their own nakedness. Physicians spared their sensitive female patients the indignity of undressing for an examination; women could point out where they hurt on a doll conveniently provided for that purpose. Even the legs of tables and pianos were modestly draped to avoid conjuring up impure thoughts.

Fortunately, not everyone went along.

During the early stages of industrialization, the artists and writers of the Romantic Movement looked back to a lost Golden Age they imagined existing before the coming of the machine. Rejecting political solutions, the Romantics still sought to fulfill the promise of the French Revolution—liberty, equality, and fraternity. But strictly in personal terms.

Shelley, Byron, Keats, George Sand, Goethe, and Beethoven are a few of the names linked with the Romantic spirit. All preferred passion to cold, analytical reason. All exalted the rights of the individual to pursue happiness. And all endorsed the idea of female equality—especially in love— over the traditional attempt to enslave women in the name of adoring or protecting them.

The Romantics had a powerful cultural influence that persists into our own time. The doomed lovers that people the popular "romances" found on stage and screen, and at the supermarket check-out counter, are the distant literary descendents of that Movement.

But to actually transform the world requires some kind of program. This the Romantics could not provide. But others of that time could and did.

Robert Owen, a successful English manufacturer, proposed that the cruel and crass materialism of the Industrial Age could only be altered by replacing individual greed with collective sharing. Accordingly, he reorganized his own factory along humane, socialist lines. But it was Owen's *social* program that drew the most criticism from the prudes in power.

In 1833, he declared that marriage without love was worse than prostitution. For this reason, Owen advocated the institution of trial marriage, as well as easier divorce. Children, a public trust, would also be cared for by the community under this system.

Owen put theory into practice by financing several experimental communities in Europe and North America. All were short-lived. New Harmony, established in Indiana by 900 settlers, began promisingly. But political arguments soon got the upper hand. The group quickly split into four separate communes—before disbanding altogether.

The most successful and longest-lived social experiment of the period was set up in Oneida, New York by John Humphrey Noyes, a radical theologian. For over 30 years—1848 to 1879—hundreds of Oneidans practiced a non-possessive sexuality called "Complex Marriage."

"The new commandment is that we love one another . . . not by pairs, as in the world, but en masse."

—*Noyes*

Noyes preached Bible Communism, a belief that when God's will was done on earth, there would be no more private property or possessive marriage.

It was also necessary to jettison the traditional Western hostility toward sex and the body. *"To be ashamed of the sex organs is to be ashamed of God's workmanship,"* he wrote.

The organization of the Oneida commune was a theocracy, with Noyes firmly in control from the pulpit. Collective farming and light industry run along socialist lines provided an unusually high standard of living for all.

The sexual life of Oneida was carefully structured. Records show that the average woman there had anywhere from two to four different lovers each week. Yet "exclusive" relationships with any one person were discouraged as a threat to group solidarity.

Sexual equality was the rule and Oneida's unique sexual practices allowed women to escape the perpetual parenthood of the outside world. Men were taught "male continence," a sexual technique which let them engage in intercourse without ejaculation. Older women trained the younger men in this system—and it was only the rare liaison that accidentally produced children.

146

Soon after, there was trouble in Paradise. By the late 1870s, Noyes had become too old and sickly to govern effectively. The younger leadership lacked the communal fervor of the first generation of Oneidans. Some even rebelled against tradition and carried on forbidden, exclusive romantic attachments.

Outside opposition from clergymen, politicians, and local vigilantes finally forced Noyes to flee to Canada for safety. By 1880, the great social experiment had come to an end.

Back in Europe, another kind of communist was also taking aim at marriage as an institution. Marriage, wrote Frederick Engels, derives its form from the economic system in which it exists.

Where wealth is shared, women are free to love at will.

148

Looking back over history, Engels realized that when private property became important, men wanted a way of passing their possessions on to their children—and not some other man's offspring. This required strict control of female sexuality. In patriarchal systems, the man assumed the role of the *owner* of the woman, her children, and all the family possessions. The result?

"The woman was degraded and reduced to servitude; she became the slave of his lust and a mere instrument for the production of children."

—*Engels*

Middle class monogamy is fraud, Engels and his comrade Karl Marx declared. Men of means have always been able to have sex with other women. But wives are kept at home, under sexual lock and key. The solution? Abolish private wealth, and you also abolish the family as an economic unit. Let the state care for all children. Allow women to become economically independent. Then, and only then, will we have long-lasting relationships based on equality and love—not possessiveness and need.

Ironically, one of the strongest attacks on the whole structure of Victorian sexuality came from a man who was relatively puritanical in his own sexual life and who believed that a certain degree of sexual repression was necessary for civilization.

Remember Sigmund Freud?

> *"I have not gained the impression that sexual abstinence helps to bring about energetic and self-reliant men of action or original thinkers or bold emancipators and reformers. Far more often it goes to produce well-behaved weaklings who later become lost in the great mass of people . . ."*

Worse, too much sexual repression could have positively uncivilized results. Freud believed that sex drive—or libido—was the natural product of a healthy organism. Early in his career, Freud realized that severely repressed patients often developed unhealthy symptoms such as tics, stuttering, paralysis, even hysteria.

Freud theorized that when the libido was blocked, it was often rechanneled into the darker, forbidden quarters of the unconscious—the repository of all desires. From there it could re-emerge in the form of aggressive, even perverted, fantasies and deeds.

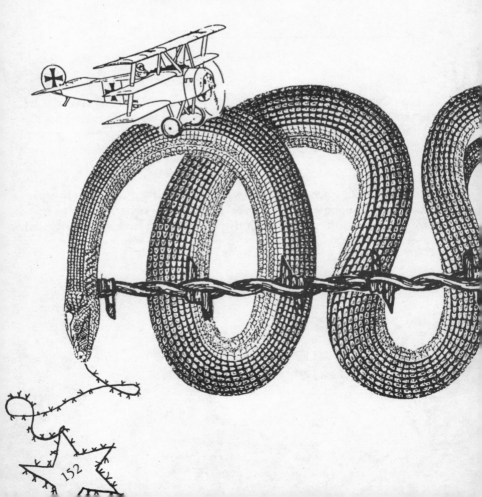

The madness of war, Freud came to believe, was caused by the Return of the Repressed ... on an international scale. What else could explain the spectacle of millions of civilized men joyfully marching to their deaths in the trenches of the Western Front? Freud concluded that the unparalled carnage of World War I was the result of excessive instinctual repression imposed upon a generation of Europeans living "beyond their moral means."

One veteran of that war was a young, socially conscious psychologist who tried forge a synthesis of Marx and Freud. His name was Wilhelm Reich.

Unlike Freud, Reich believed that sexual neurosis was not inevitable. But both men agreed on the place where people first learned repression: *The Family*.

Reich viewed the hierarchy of the family as a model for other oppressive social systems. More than that, the family was also . . .

"A factory for authoritarian ideologies and conservative structures . . ."
—*Reich*

In this particular factory, children are conditioned to obey authority and clamp down on their own feelings. Early sexual play, naturally, is one of the first areas of conflict.

154

*C*hildren's genital experimentation is usually dealt with by punishment, humiliation, deprivation of affection, and threats.

*F*or Reich, this crippling of spontaneous sexual expression leads to a paralysis of the child's entire personality. Once and for all, the child's spirit is broken. He or she is now ready to be molded into a cog in an oppressive social machine.

*E*urope in the 20s and 30s provided an extreme example of this process: Nazi Germany. Stiff uniforms, regimented salutes, heel clicking, goose steps, mass formations, and public spectacles. There, sexual energy was channeled into war production and military training. Natural aggressive instincts were perverted into a national cult of sadomasochism and death.

Reich believed that even under less extreme conditions, the individual i modern Western civilization adjusts to an environment of repression by develop ing physical and emotional defenses.

"In the conflict between instinct and morals, ego and outer world, the organism is forced to armor itself."

—Rei

b l a b l a b l a b

Reich believed that body armor could not be dissolved by Freud's "talking cure" alone. Physical methods also had to be employed to teach the self to respond to touch, to emotions, and to the complete surrender of the orgasm. It wasn't enough for the individual to understand the causes of his or her own neurosis. To get well, he or she must actually learn how to satisfy sexual needs.

Body armor takes the forms of muscular rigidness, defensive postures, and a habitually deadened response to inner and outer sensation. Armor protects t fragile self, but exacts a terrible price: it cuts the individual off from t experience of pleasure.

During the 1920s, Reich excitedly watched the social experimentation taking place under the Bolsheviks in the Soviet Union. Total equality between the sexes was officially proclaimed. The revolutionary government made birth control, abortion, and easy divorce available for all. To a limited extent, the economic functions of the family were replaced by the State, which took responsibility for feeding, housing, and caring for children.

With the rise of Stalin in the late 1920s, traditional attitudes toward the family, sex, and the sexes returned to Russia. Reich, however, continued to believe in the need for a vast socio-sexual transformation in Europe.

Accordingly, he helped to create sex clinics for working people in Austria and Germany. And he actively supported birth control and abortion—two measures he believed removed some of the fear from sex.

157

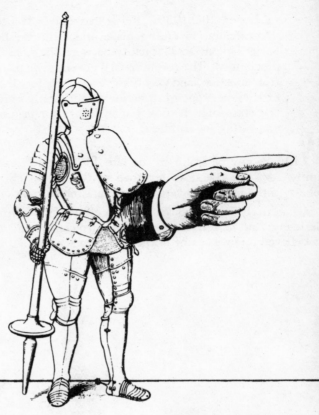

Yet in the partisan 1930s, Reich found himself increasingly alienated from th
orthodox followers of both Marx and Freud. He was first kicked out of th
Communist Party for writing his controversial book, "The Mass Psychology c
Fascism," which strongly criticized Stalinist Russia. Shortly after, he was als
expelled from Freud's International Psychoanalytic Association.

Reich moved on. Eventually, he wound up as a wartime refugee in America
Here he became less interested in the social and psychological dimensions c
sexuality. And more concerned with studying sex as a biological and physica
process.

Increasingly, Reich began to reduce things to the level of sexual physics. Even the orgasm—which he claimed was the key to health—was now defined as "a phenomenon of electrical discharge." Perhaps he had discovered the scientific base of the ancient sex practices of the Taoists and Tantrists. Or perhaps, as many opponents claimed, he had succumbed to mysticism and gone mad.

Mad or not, Reich's ideas eventually attracted a wide audience in America. H
mystical concepts linking the body with the energy of the cosmos were quick
adopted by the Beats in the 1950s and the hippies in the 1960s. Many psych
therapists today also value Reich's work with breaking down body armor.

ut Reich's earlier, political writings also had a tremendous effect. In 1948, uthor George Orwell published a novel which told of a future society dom- nated by the principles of mass psychology as outlined by Reich. The book was alled . . .

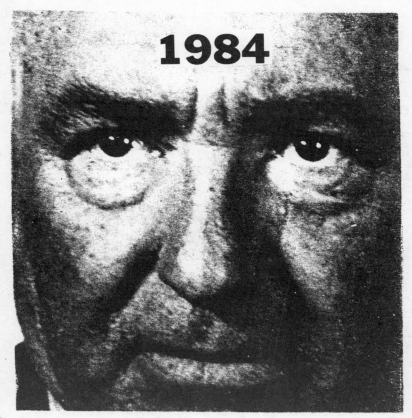

1984

Orwell painted a terrifying portrait of a totalitarian state perpetually at war, of people incapable of individual thought and feeling—uniformed, mobilized, nd harnessed to a relentless industrial machine. Repressed libido was the fuel hat powered this war state. And as Reich might've predicted, here sex was the ltimate crime.

In the industrial West, obviusly, the future turned out significantly different rom what Orwell had foretold. And that future—which is our present *today*— happened first in the United States of America.

The Age of Desire

x x o x o o x x o o o x x o x x o o x

"Sex: in America an obsession. In other parts of the world, a fact."

—*Marlene Dietrich*

The year was 1955, the place the good ole USA. A bald-headed war hero, Dwight Eisenhower, was the nation's father figure. Right-wing Senator Joe McCarthy was still leading a well-publicized witch hunt against dirty reds and homos in high places. The puritanical Citizens for Decent Literature, with the support of many clergymen, were busy sniffing out smutty books and movies in low places.

And for most teenagers, the only place to learn about the human anatomy was *National Geographic*.

It was a time when nice girls didn't. Or if they did, they didn't talk about it. Birth control, abortion, and even sex education were illegal or unavailable in most parts of the country. On TV and in the movies, married couples could only be shown sleeping in separate beds. And while screen stars tried to titilate audiences with low cut clothes that revealed more than they concealed, the underlying message of American culture in that period seemed to be:

Look, but don't touch.

163

$\mathcal{J}$ust fifteen years later, in 1970, the sexual environment seemed to have changed dramatically. America was in the middle of an erotic explosion that many would call the Sexual Revolution.

$\mathfrak{B}$irth control became more available. Sex education became a part of the school curriculum. Pre-marital and extra-marital sex became more acceptable. Divorce became easier to obtain.

Traditional monogamous marriage had to compete with new forms such as group and "open marriage," communal sex, "swinging" and spouse swapping. Social nudity became tolerated in private and in public situations such as the beach, outdoor festivals, and protests. Films and publications became more explicit. And sexual research and therapy became widespread.

Why? There is no simple answer. But here are some of the pieces of the puzzle.

Sexual Research

Dr. Alfred C. Kinsey's reports on Male Sexual Behavior (1948) and Female Sexual Behavior (1953) began to penetrate the general American consciousness in the mid-Fifties. At that time, their main effect was to convince millions that most people were much more sexually active than anyone had ever acknowledged before.

Kinsey was a conservative, highly respectable zoologist who specialized in insects. When asked to teach sex education at Indiana University, he discovered that science knew more about the love life of bugs than it knew about people. To compile his reports, Kinsey questioned more than 10,000 men and women over a decade. Here are some of his startling results:

Masturbation—Almost 95% of all males and roughly two-thirds of all females admitted to practicing it. Figures were highest for younger and unmarried men. Women who masturbated, the report claimed, were far more likely to experience orgasm in intercourse.

Extramarital Sex—Half of all men in the study had intercourse at least occasionally with women other than their wives. 25% of women reported extramarital relations in their thirties and early forties.

Homosexuality—More than one man in three reported at least one homosexual experience leading to orgasm. 13% claimed to be predominantly gay. For women, 28% stated that they'd had at least one homosexual experience by middle age.

The Kinsey Reports—like the research done later by Masters and Johnson—made sex a respectable topic for discussion. Equally important, many Americans learned that they were not alone in having powerful sexual desires.

The Supreme Court

In 1938, the New York Board of Censors banned all movies that mentioned pregnancy, venereal disease, birth control, abortion, illegitimacy, prostitution, inter-racial sex, and divorce. Yet nineteen years later, in 1957, the US Supreme Court made a historic decision that would overturn this kind of censorship in both visual and written material.

According to the Court, books and magazines for adults could no longer be banned in order to supposedly protect children from viewing them. In a related decision, the Court also ruled in ROTH vs US that obscene materials had to be utterly without redeeming social value before they could be banned. The effect of these decisions was to end prosecution of literary works, erotic art, and "soft core" pornography.

Justice William O. Douglas would later explain the changing view of the Court as follows:

"The idea of using obscenity to bar thoughts of sex is dangerous. A person without sex thoughts is abnormal. Sex thoughts may induce sex practices that make for better marital relations. Sex thoughts that make love attractive certainly should not be outlawed."

Extended Adolescence & Leisure Time

After the sacrifices of the Great Depression (1929–1938) and World War most Americans wanted a chance to enjoy the benefits of post-War prosperity more positive attitude toward leisure was an important psychological factor the acceptance of "recreational sex."

Greater industrial productivity cut the work week to five days. This left m time for leisure—which became a major industry by the 1960s. Expenditures recreation and cultural activities more than doubled within a decade, a rate growth considerably larger than that of the US gross national product.

The "extended adolescence" of higher education also helped to create a n leisure class of young college people. From 1954 to 1970, the percentage Americans in college doubled from 16% to 32%. In most cases, it was this gro who first replaced the puritan notion of delayed gratification with the mode ideal of SATISFACTION NOW. But the rest of American society was soon follow.

Decline of Religion

Organized religion declined in numbers and influence during the 1950s and 0s. As Americans lost interest in traditional creeds, the old sexual morals also me under attack.

The nation was becoming better educated. In 1940, the average person had /2 years of school. By 1970, it was up to 12 years. These people refused to cept Church doctrine blindly. Liberalized laws on birth control, abortion, and xual activities also caused a crisis of conscience among many believers.

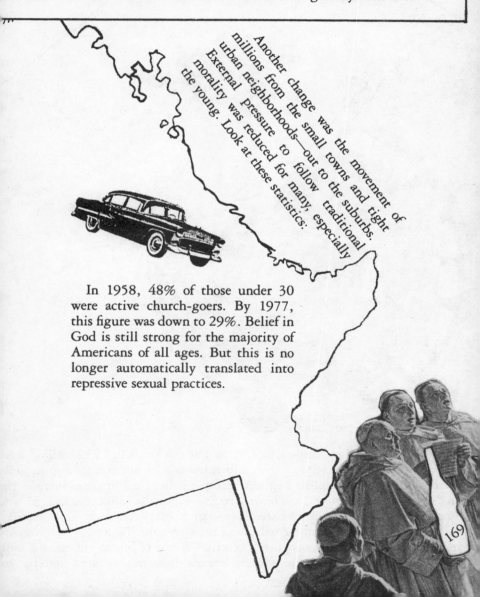

Another change was the movement of millions from the small towns and tight urban neighborhoods—out to the suburbs. External pressure to follow traditional morality was reduced for many, especially the young. Look at these statistics:

In 1958, 48% of those under 30 were active church-goers. By 1977, this figure was down to 29%. Belief in God is still strong for the majority of Americans of all ages. But this is no longer automatically translated into repressive sexual practices.

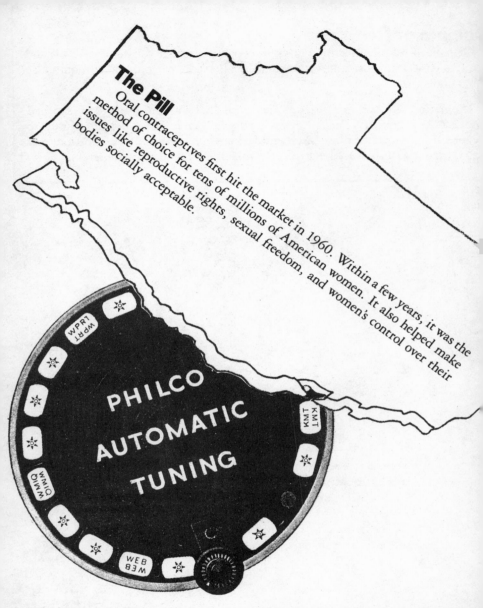

The Pill

Oral contraceptives first hit the market in 1960. Within a few years, it was the method of choice for tens of millions of American women. It also helped make issues like reproductive rights, sexual freedom, and women's control over their bodies socially acceptable.

The Pill—like the intrauterine devices first marketed in 1959—allowed for more spontaneity and delicacy than traditional condoms and diaphragms. Only in the 1970s did researchers begin to recognize that the Pill could increase the risk of blood clots, strokes, and heart attacks—especially for women over 35 who smoke. Yet the Pill also seems to reduce certain kinds of cancer, pelvic inflammatory diseases, excessive menstrual bleeding, and arthritis. Even though many have switched to safer—though less certain—forms of contraception, the long popularity of the Pill helped remove the fear of unwanted pregnancy from the sex lives of a generation.

Television

The growth of tv in this period not only spread many of these important changes through America. The medium itself was a powerful force in the "sexualization" of American life and culture.

The number of tv sets jumped from 33 million in 1955 to nearly 80 million in 1969. The percentages of homes with tv in this period increased from 67% to 95%. For most Americans, television became the number One source of entertainment and news.

Despite official "standards" of decency, tv dramas and comedies increasingly relied on a frothy mix of sex, romance, and violence to attract viewers. Advertisers depended on sex and romance for much the same reasons.

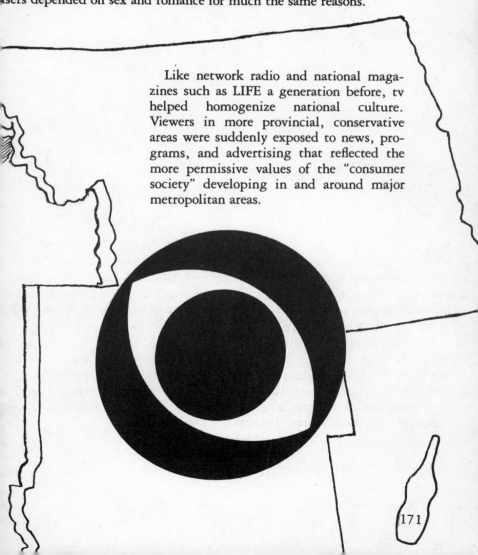

Like network radio and national magazines such as LIFE a generation before, tv helped homogenize national culture. Viewers in more provincial, conservative areas were suddenly exposed to news, programs, and advertising that reflected the more permissive values of the "consumer society" developing in and around major metropolitan areas.

The Profit Motive

This is the force that really drove the Sexual Revolution. Many of the chan~~ges~~ that took place in the period 1955–1970 would have been extremely limited ~~in~~ effect—if they couldn't have been exploited for commercial purposes.

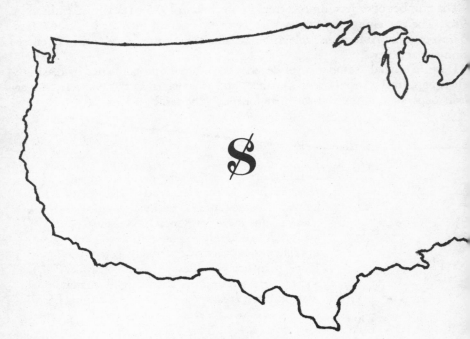

Mass market magazines were quick to see the sensationalistic side of Kinse~~y's~~ sober sociological reports. Drug manufacturers launched multi-million dollar ~~ad~~ campaigns to alert American women to the benefits of The Pill and the IU~~D.~~ Movie companies rapidly capitalized on the new sexual openness, as did clothi~~ng~~ designers and swim suit makers.

But we can see the naked profit motive most clearly in the area of obsceni~~ty.~~ When the Supreme Court permitted erotica with redeeming social content, ~~it~~ was likely thinking in terms of the books of James Joyce, Henry Miller, and Alle~~n~~ Ginsberg. Since that time, however, a multibillion dollar porno industry h~~as~~ grown up around the sale of publications, movies, and videos. There—~~not~~ literature—is where the real market seems to have been.

From the perspective of 1970, it was only natural to ask where the American-ation of sex would lead. What would the next 15 years of the Sexual Revolution roduce? Would a sexually satisfied nation find it easier to make love, not war? Would new, more creative relationships develop between people?

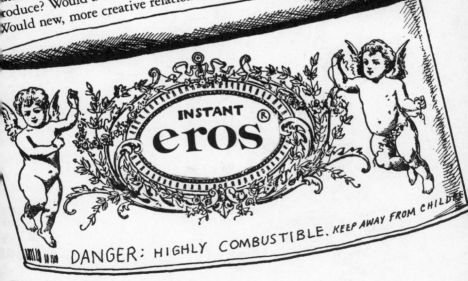

INSTANT
eros ®

DANGER: HIGHLY COMBUSTIBLE. *KEEP AWAY FROM CHILD*

Or would the Americanization of sex bring our bodies together but leave the rest of our lives as unfulfilled as before? Could Eros thrive in an environment that packaged and marketed sex like any other product?

Now, from our vantage point in the 1980s, we still find ourselves asking so[m]
of the same questions. The main difference is that we today are in a bet[ter]
position to assess the Sexual Revolution, its successes and failures. And we [are]
also forced to ask whether or not there is a future for that Revolution. Or has [it]
already come and gone, its message smoothed out, tucked in, toned down, a[nd]
cut up to fit the format of a TV screen or centerfold spread?

Don't touch that dial! We'll be right back with answers to these and other intriguing questions after a timely message about supply and demand.

Until 200 years ago, most of Europe and America lived as the majority of the world still lives: in the country or in small villages. People grew or made what they needed, and traded the surplus. The average person saw him or herself as part of something larger—a village, a clan, a family. Sexual morality came from local interpretation of the Bible, which might be quite savage in some situations. Industrialization changed all that.

Peasants who left the land for the new factory towns discovered that they had escaped the old ways forever. Now they were strangers, on their own, with no snoopy relatives, neighbors, or local ministers to account to. True, they had also lost their sense of belonging to something—but they were now individuals, free to seek what pleasures they could afford on skimpy factory wages.

There was no turning back. Some clergymen complained that industrialization increased immorality by removing the old social controls. Husbands abandoned the family and the farm, never to return. Working women were exposed to numerous temptations on the job and off. Grandparents were left back on the old sod, to fend for themselves. Children were growing up on the dirty streets, with no adult to care for them. Drunkenness, gambling, and dancing spread like a plague. Church attendance dropped, with no one to enforce it. Making money was all anybody thought about.

Do some of these charges sound familiar today?

Karl Marx studied the industrial forces that dominated the lives of these working people. He noticed that the economy seemed to go through regular cycles of boom and bust. Technology could produce an ever-increasing supply of goods for sale. But it took time for old products to wear out, and for people to save up for new purchases. For this reason, the demand for new products seemed to grow at a slower rate than the potential supply.

Economic depressions, Marx theorized, are caused chiefly by this glut in productivity. When the market is saturated, demand drops.

This causes manufacturers to cut production. Plants close, workers get laid off, wages drop, and companies compete fiercely for the remaining market. Eventually, industry giants and outright monopolies dominate the economy.

Marx predicted that these business cycles would grow harsher over time, leaving wealth in fewer and fewer hands. Impoverished workers would ultimately see the need for total revolutionary change.

177

But what Marx couldn't have predicted was that demand for new products could be manufactured almost as easily as the products themselves. How?

- **Credit**—encourage people to buy now, pay later.
- **Planned Obsolescence**—design products to wear out sooner than necessary.
- **Advertising**—stimulate people to desire the new, improved goods constantly pouring out of the factories.

The result of this process was the creation of a Consumer Society in which wealth is no longer valued for its own sake—as a mark of status, power, and security. For most of us today, wealth is valued as a means to enjoy the good things of life. In short, all that money can buy.

What is the connection between sexual and social relations in a society dominated by the Consumption Ethic? What is modern life like today in the Age of Desire?

All of us have a strong need to be loved, respected, and valued by others.

Advertising does not create these needs. But advertising does *focus* on these needs to generate personal desires.

But let's examine the needs that ads exploit so effectively, beginning with one that's often overlooked: the need for Autonomy—a sense of being in control over one's own life.

---

150 years ago, 90% of all Americans worked for themselves as farmers, craftspersons, shopkeepers, fishermen, and so on. By 1950, the percentage of self-employed was down to 18%. Ten years later, the figure was 14%. And in 1970, only 9% of the population worked for themselves.

What this trend shows is that fewer Americans than ever are in a position to decide what kind of work they will do, what they produce—how, when, where, why, and for whom?

These important decisions are increasingly made by those who own and run the giant corporations and institutions that run the country.

What this means is that for most of us, the need for autonomy and control is usually satisfied outside the workplace. And what this often comes down to is the freedom to choose what we will or will not consume, in the form of products to buy and leisure activities—including sex—to enjoy.

As social critic Chris Lasch puts it:

> *"Is your job boring and meaningless? Does it leave you with feelings of futility and fatigue? Is your life empty? Consumption promises to fill the aching void; hence the attempt to surround commodities with an aura of romance, with allusions to exotic places and vivid experiences; and with images of female breasts from which all blessings flow."*
> —*Christopher Lasch*

Sex is used in advertising for two main reasons:

DR. EDWARDS'
Olive Tablets
THE LAXATIVE
OF BEAUTIFUL WOMEN

To attract attention.

It is pleasant to look upon what gives us pleasure. Using a sexy image to market an unsexy product or service is called "borrowed interest."

o create positive identifications.

Think of Pavlov's dog. It was trained to associate a ringing bell with feeding, and could be made to salivate on demand. In a more sophisticated way, ads condition consumers to identify specific goods with feelings of pleasure, romance and satisfaction. One way to do this is through **motivational design.**

In other words, design the rear end of a car to look like the rear end of a woman, and the bumpers to look like breasts—and the car will seem sexier to look at and drive. Auto companies, in fact, were the first to use sex in designing car bodies and ad strategies. Today sexual symbolism is also found in a vast array of other products.

Another important advertising technique uses words and expressions with double—usually sexual—meanings. In a single issue of LIFE magazine, for example, 26 ads featured the word "come" in their pitch.

"Come up and see SEX for BEGINNERS some time !!"

Double meanings, naturally, are also found in the way ads position people and objects in a shot.

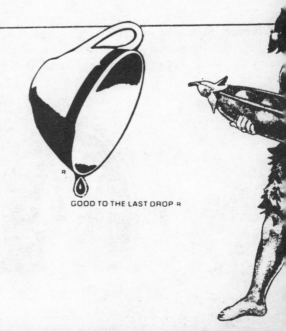

GOOD TO THE LAST DROP R

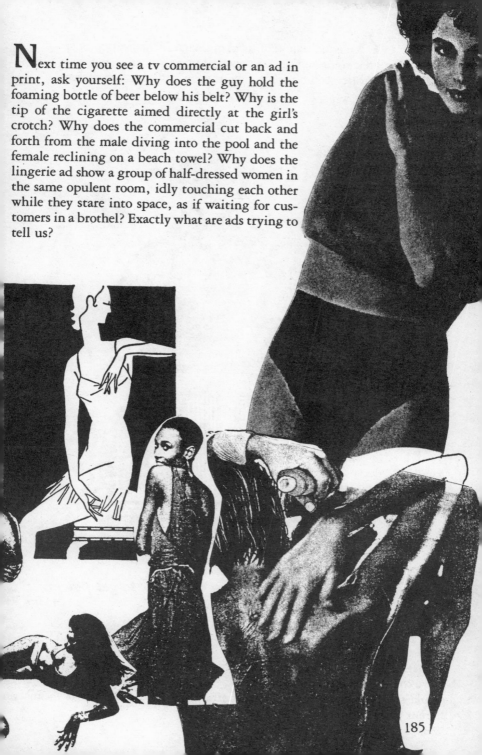

Next time you see a tv commercial or an ad in print, ask yourself: Why does the guy hold the foaming bottle of beer below his belt? Why is the tip of the cigarette aimed directly at the girl's crotch? Why does the commercial cut back and forth from the male diving into the pool and the female reclining on a beach towel? Why does the lingerie ad show a group of half-dressed women in the same opulent room, idly touching each other while they stare into space, as if waiting for customers in a brothel? Exactly what are ads trying to tell us?

An equally potent form of sexual identification operates right out in the open, but it is connected to a public secret people in our officially classless society only whisper about: *STATUS.*

"Men use power to get sex. Women use sex to get power."

—Tom Wo

Whether this generalization is morally right or wrong, and whether or not yo believe the situation is changing rapidly—on Madison Avenue, reporter Wolf formula still holds true. Status is definitely linked to sex, but it means ver different things to each of the sexes.

Among animals and throughout human history, high status individuals have always had their pick of mating partners. High status apes, one example, are usually the biggest, smartest or most ferocious. In our society, male status is a product of social power, wealth—and only secondarily, physical strength and appearance. After all,

t is the high status males who set the standards.

187

Traditionally, females have been forced to achieve wealth and power through men in their lives. Youth and sexual appeal, combined with calculating intelligence, are what ambitious women have usually needed to attain the comfort, security, glory and luxury that men customarily receive from personal success.

Advertising expertly utilizes these dual status systems to create desires from needs:

Men shown with the trappings of wealth and status are rewarded with sexually desirable women. Sexually desirable women, in turn, are rewarded by being shown with high status men. This simple formula reappears over and over each day as the "happy ending" which results from using product after product.

Ads didn't create status anxiety, sexual competition, or dissatisfaction with oneself and one's position in the world. But advertising continually capitalizes these concerns, magnifies them, and reminds us of them in a significant perc of the . . .

14.2 billion newspaper ads

1.4 billion magazine ads

730,000 radio commercials

190

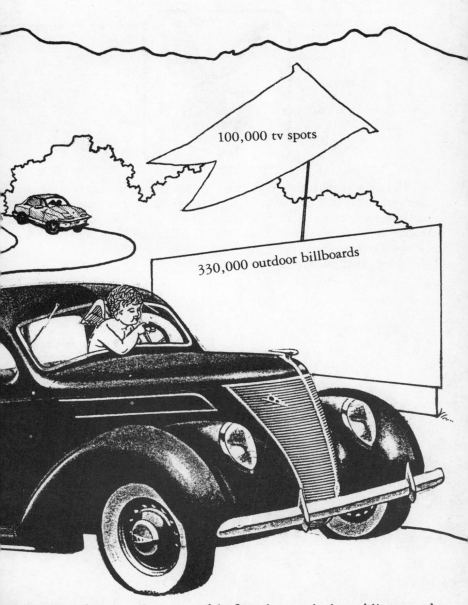

100,000 tv spots

330,000 outdoor billboards

d 51 million direct mail pieces and leaflets that reach the public every day.
eoples Almanac, page 808, 1975)

Saturation advertising has transformed the environment of our homes, neighborhoods, cities, and highways into an everexpanding landscape of desire.

But has the habit of desire also affected our sexual needs and fantasies? Y[ou] decide.

Playboy is a publication dedicated to the continuing appeal of the hi[gh] consumption Good Life. Women in this magazine are shown as one of t[he] rewards of success, along with new cars, clothes, and electronic gadgets. Pla[y] mates are depicted as an endless assortment of delightful bon bons to be devour[ed] anew every month. And the magazine's fetish for huge female breasts is just o[ne] of the things that put the boy back in *Playboy*.

"I feel like a kid in the world's biggest candystore."
—*Hugh Heffner*

The success of magazines like this does not depend upon any lack of sexual opportunity in our society. Instead, their success is the result of a certain familiar psychological reality. Author Raphael Patai explains:

"The average, ordinary man can have sexual intercourse with women . . . but the women whom he can enjoy are, of necessity, his own female counterparts: in other words, average, ordinary women."

Having such women, may satisfy a man's sexual hunger, but not his erotic fantasies. In these fantasies, a man can imagine himself conquering and possessing the most beautiful, attractive, and sexually desirable examples of the opposite sex.

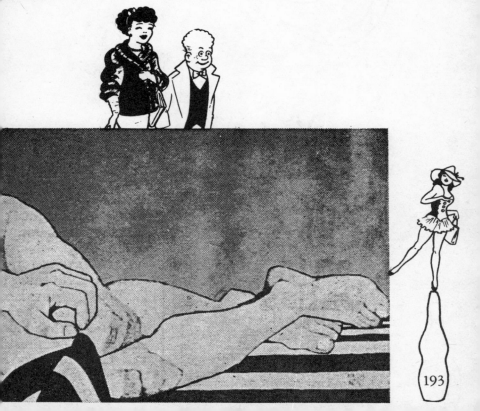

Another kind of sexual fantasy is found in the pages of popular women's magazines. Covers, photos, articles, ads, and even the horoscope all send the same message: that a woman's reward for making herself attractive is sweet surrender to the right man.

Unlike the male emphasis on what you must own or accomplish to be a winner in the sexual sweepstakes, *Cosmopolitan* and *Vogue* and the others focus on what you must do to yourself to be more desirable:

Cosmo

DON'T BLOW IT!
curb flatulence on your honeymoon!

white out BLACKHEADS
forever!

Double D is ALL OVER BUSTING OUT
(big girls don't cry)
p. 88

194

elle

NEW!
Anorexic Diet Tips
P. 11

Pisces **A**dvicies:
fishing for complements
without getting fried

healthy skins
Leather Virgins
tell all!!
P. 69

YOU DON'T HAVE
TO BE JEWISH
to be a "J.A.P."

(P.S. And neither does he —
so buyer beware!)

195

The rules of romance were first set down 800 years ago at the Court of Love presided over by the remarkable French Queen, Eleanor. But there is much in them that holds true today—as can be seen in this declaration by Eleanor's court poet, Andreas Capellanus:

"Everybody knows that love can have no place between husband and wife. They may be bound to each other by a great and immoderate affection, but their feeling cannot take the place of love . . ."

Why?

Because romantic love gains power and passion from the obstacles in its path. Andreas defines it as an overwhelming desire to passionately exchange hidden, forbidden embraces. But what embrace can be forbidden between husband and wife? They have a right to each other. And what is obligatory cannot be given freely.

Romance was conceived in a time when marriages were arranged and divorce was practically impossible. It developed as a formula for adulterous love. But in our time—when people are free to marry and divorce—it is too often a recipe for failure.

A glance at any of today's women's publications will show the difficulty of sustaining romance in the face of the real world.

197

The romantic myth makes us want to believe that somewhere, out there, there is a person who is our perfect soulmate for all time. All we have to do is wade through enough people and we'll find our shining star.

With so many sexual opportunities available to us today, why dwell on fantasies? Or is there something missing in our relationships that fantasies supply?

Have we become a society of erotic consumers? Are we so attracted to the packaging and appearance of our love objects that we fail to study the fine print? When a relationship has dulled or tarnished, are we inclined to just throw it away or trade it in for a newer model? Is planned obsolescence also a part of our erotic lives?

Half of all American marriages begun this year will end in divorce. For many of us, the old straight-laced monogamy has given way to a new kind of polygamy: serial marriage. Divorce follows divorce like the changing seasons of the heart. Do we marry for the wrong reasons? Is the family an outmoded concept? Do the media myths of sexual conquest and surrender sabotage our blind groping toward love? Has our ability to make any longterm commitments whatsoever fallen victim to the instant gratifications of the Age of Desire?

Has sex itself become a substitute for other interests? Other challenges? Other ways of relating to the world?

What else would explain, in the words of Edmund White,

"the cry for scorching, multiple orgasms, the drive toward impeccable and virtuoso performance, the belief that only in complete sexual compatibility lies true intimacy, the insistence that sex is the only mode for experiencing thrills, for achieving love, for assessing and demonstrating personal worth?"

Is it possible, that today's sexual obsession is at least partly the result of a general feeling of powerlessness? In other words, people believe they can no longer have an effect on the world, but at least they have some say over who they court and sleep with.

What is the future of relationships in the Age of Desire? The Industrial Revolution put an end to the extended farm family—

201

Will our technologically advanced post-industrial society also put an end to the nuclear family—mom, dad, and 2.5 kids under the same split-level roof? Will the one-parent family become the rule?

Since 1970, the number of American men living alone has doubled. Is th growing Singles Lifestyle a real alternative? The number of single and divorce women living on their own are also increasing. To serve this segment of th population, the Loneliness Industry was created.

It supplies singles bars, resorts, vacations, magazines, dating clubs, an housing developments. Witness the spread of expensive single-portion conve nience foods, small studio apartments, and the avalanche of other goods an services directed at this group's needs, desires, anxieties, and search for compar ionship. Even the current sporting rage—jogging—is tailored to the indeper dent single person.

It's easy to mock an over-ambitious Yuppie. But what's so bad about living fo yourself? Call it selfishness, narcissism, alienation, or whatever—

ood question. The hopes of free lovers and revolutionaries throughout history have been based on establishing communities of free selves who form relationships on the principles of choice and shared need—not compulsion. The bottom line is that no one should be forced into relationships he or she doesn't want. But what about those of us who desperately want loving relationships—and find ourselves stymied at every turn?

Today we have many of the freedoms that sexual revolutionaries of the past only dreamed about. Yet too often there is something missing from the equation. Something that robs us of the possibilities for happiness. Something that keeps us isolated from each other, restless and ready for the next fad or fashion that promises to put our lives together for us. That missing something is a sense of shared community.

Erotic relationships, as Freud pointed out, are the model for other carin
relationships in a society. We know there is plenty of room for sex in the Age c
Desire. But is there any place left for Eros—the force that brings us together

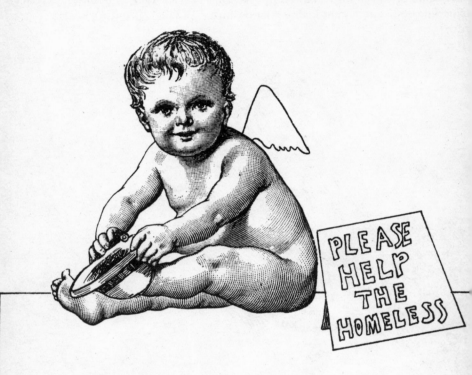

In our competitive society, individual is pitted against individual in the
struggle for survival. Success brings unparallelled freedom and affluence for the
lucky few. But rich or poor, we all live in a world not completely of our own
making. Problems such as crime, pollution, war, racism, sexism, disease, and
the suffering of our neighbors affect all of us.

Individual solutions are simply inadequate. Our world is too complex. And escape is only a temptation mirage.

Some say that society will change if we change the way we deal with each other,

if we become more loving, more caring.

Others reply unless we alter the structure of society,

any change in personal relations will be manipulated by those who profit from our most basic needs.

And yet others want to turn the clock back completely. The Moral Majority and other ultra-conservative groups still believe that sex is a dirty word. Who can say for sure the best path for each person to take out of the Age of Desire?

Some even wonder if it's a good thing to ask questions about sex at all.

Why complicate such a simple matter?

eople who feel this way often refer to the popular myth about Eros and the beautiful mortal, Psyche, whose name means soul in Greek. According to the myth, Eros whisked the girl away to a palace on a mountaintop. The young god came to her at night and together they made perfect love. There was a catch, however. Eros warned Psyche that she must never look upon his face.

Curiosity got the better of her, though. After a bout of love, when the young god slumbered next to her in bed, Psyche held an oil lamp up to his face. She marveled at his beauty. But a drop of hot oil fell on Eros. He awoke instantly and fled.

The moral of the tale, at least according to some people, is that when love is examined too closely it disappears. But wait! There is a final part of the myth that many are unaware of.

After Eros fled, Psyche realized her loss. She tried to take her own life, but the fates intervened. Her suffering moved the gods themselves on Olympus. They agreed to give poor Psyche immortality. Together, joined as equals, Eros and Psyche were allowed at last to live together in peace and bliss.

*And if it's possible
for them, why not for us?*

Afterword:
The Death of Sex?

"For my loins are filled with a loathesome disease; and there is no soundness in my flesh."

—38th Psalm

Will the threat of AIDS (Acquired Immune Deficiency Syndrome) put an end to the Age of Desire? Who can say for sure. What is certain is that this mysterious epidemic will certainly affect the way we live out our desires in years to come.

Not all epidemics are the same. The devastations of typhus or bubonic plague, for example, were often passed by one person to many people at once. What could an individual do to protect him or herself, except perhaps to withdraw completely from human contact? And even then there were no guarantees.

Aids, fortunately, is another matter. Like other sexually transmitted diseases, it is both a medical problem and a social phenomenon. The disease is not contracted through fleas, lice, airborne microbes, or tainted food. Aids is spread by the way people live and love—one individual at a time. When we modify our behavior, we clearly reduce the risk.

Will Aids effect the future of sex? It's far too early to know with certainty. Yet to gain some kind of perspective on the disease and its impact, it may be helpful to examine a terrible sexual epidemic of the past: syphilis.

Today, most of us consider syphilis a relatively minor matter that can be cleared up by repeated doses of penicillin or other antibiotics. Yet for over four centuries, contracting the disease was the same thing as receiving a death sentence.

Syphilis, like Aids today, suddenly seemed to appear on the scene. In the year 1492, for reasons still unknown, the French army beseiging the city of Naples came down with a deadly new disease—or a virulent form of an old disease people had acquired some immunity to. Then as now, syphilis had three stages.

In the first, a hard chancre appears on the infected genitals. Next the skin breaks out in the lesions or *postules* that gave the disease its common name—the pox. In the final stage, the victim suffers various afflictions of the bones, muscles, intestines, and nervous system. In the end is only madness and death.

A year after the first outbreak, the Emperor Maximillian warned of a new epidemic "which had never occurred before nor had been heard of within the memory of man." He believed that the cause of the pox was God's punishment for blasphemy—religious impiety—not sexual misconduct.

Whatever its cause, syphilis spread rapidly throughout Europe.

No one knew what caused it. Some blamed an unfavorable astrological conjunction of Saturn, Jupiter, and Mars. Another theory claimed that Columbus and his crew picked up the infection in the New World and conveyed it to the Old. Current research tends to disprove this.

Closer to the truth was Alexander Benedict, an Italian who declared in 1496 that syphilis was "a new plague . . . contracted by lying together." By 1546, the word "contagion" was being used to describe the disease. Its transmission was explained in terms of tiny "seeds" or "germs" which no one, obviously, could see. No one, in fact, would see the corkscrew-shaped spirochette bacteria that cause syphilis until the year 1905.

Medical treatment of the pox was usually severe and always ineffective. Fasting and strict diets were often recommended. Strange ointments containing lard, turpentine, and mercury were applied to body lesions. This use of mercury (quicksilver or quacksilver as it was known then) is the source of our word for a medical charlatan—a quack doctor.

Not until Gabriel Fallopius invented a linen penis sheath in 1560 was there any even partially effective method of protection. A similar device, the latex condom, is still recommended today for the practice of safer sex.

When medicine failed, social remedies were undertaken. Foreigners with the pox were barred from entering France. In Scotland all those with the disease had to leave the realm or be branded on the cheek with a hot iron. In other parts of Europe, rich syphilitics were ordered to stay within their homes. The poor, treated with far less delicacy, were driven away, threatened with death, and sometimes abandoned by their doctors, who feared contracting the disease during treatment.

213

The harshest methods were reserved for prostitutes. Brothels, which had been tolerated for centuries as a necessary social evil, were now closed all over the continent. Prostitutes were driven out of city after city by the lash and the promise of life imprisonment. But since these professionals were not the only ones who carried syphilis, the disease continued its deadly spread.

Like Aids, syphilis attacked rich and poor alike. Along with hundreds of thousands of forgotten victims over the centuries, here is a partial list of some of the notable people who seem to have contracted the disease: the Dutch philosopher Erasamus, artist Albrecht Durer, sculptor Benvenuto Cellini, English King Henry VIII, playwright Jean-Baptiste Moliere, author and adventurer Gionvanni Casanova, biographer James Boswell, Czar Peter the Great, Emperor Napoleon Bonaparte, artist Francisco Goya, poet John Keats, philosopher Arthur Schopenhaur, composer Franz Schubert, poet Heinrich Heine, philosopher Friedrich Nietzsche, painter Paul Gauguin, writer Oscar Wilde, and Lord Randolph Churchill, father of Winston.

Ignorance and fear accompany every epidemic. Syphilis was no exception. In 1788, the government of Denmark took the bold step of proclaiming that: "Every person, rich or poor, suffering from a venereal disease should receive free

medical advice, free medicine, together with free nursing . . ." Free testing was also part of the plan.

In a convulsion of hysteria, a hundred decent citizens attacked one of the government clinics, armed with whips and clubs, and reportedly "foaming with rage and threatening us; if we did not leave their women and children alone, they told us, they would do violence to us . . ."

An exasperated physician on the scene complained, "In this way the disease will never be eradicated."

This sad confession brings us up to date. Sexual epidemics have a particular horror for many people, combining the legitimate fear of infection with a whole constellation of subconscious dread surrounding the sex act, eroticism, and bodily pollution. Many of us had these concerns long before anyone ever heard of Aids. And religious notions about divine retribution for sexual immorality have only compounded the anxiety.

So what should be done? The first thing is to know the facts. Aids is contracted by the exchange of body fluids, through sex, hypodermic drug use, or blood transfusion. In other words, it is spread by the things we do with and to our bodies. This fact gives us a certain degree of control.

Other weapons needed to combat Aids are sex education in the school, sexual frankness at home, accelerated research and testing, the use of condoms for the prevention of disease, and a more wary attitude toward casual sex between strangers. The real solution requires knowledge and caution, not fire and brimstone.

Hysteria is no help either. There is not even one recorded case of Aids being transmitted by casual contact—touching, sharing the same space, or even light kissing. Yet many people live in terror of contracting the disease in this way. In the process, they torment themselves and their neighbors unnecessarily.

And official hysteria only drives people further into isolation. After years of ignoring Aids or insisting it was something that only affected homosexuals—remember the term Gay Plague—today's media is filled with sensational scare stories about the spread of the disease. Maybe a strong dose of fear is necessary to build the public support needed to adequately fund research against Aids. Maybe it will help the heterosexual population at large to identify more closely with the victims of the disease, homosexual and otherwise. And maybe some people really do need to be shocked into conducting a more cautious sex life. Maybe.

Will Aids kill Eros? Not at all. But it will force Eros to make some changes. In the years following the outbreak of syphilis in Europe, the emerging Protestant movement placed great emphasis on the joys of marital love. In the Era of Aids, we should expect some similar discovery of the erotic possibilities inherent in long term relationships. This doesn't necessarily mean that sex will again be the prisoner of marriage. Men and women are more equal today than in the past;

they are also more sexually sophisticated. It's fair to assume that many couples will be able to find greater satisfaction together for longer periods of time. And why should this experience be any less gratifying than the one night stands and sexual merry go round of the last decade?

What then is the future of Eros in the Era of Aids? An effective vaccine may become available by the early 1990s. Until then, we have to protect ourselves and those we love. Our very lives depend on it. Yet who can deny that this same sense of caring is a product of erotic attraction in its fullest sense?

Remember that syphilis lasted four centuries before a cure was developed. In that time, civilization continued and actually flourished. People still fell in love, had romances, raised families, wrote love sonnets, created erotic works of art, experimented with every possible variety of sexuality, and even dreamed of a time in which total sexual liberation would be a reality.

The erotic revolutionaries of the past struggled for the kinds of changes that can't be reversed by any virus. The sexual freedom they envisioned includes equality between the sexes—in bed, on the job, and elsewhere. This freedom is expressed by the demand of the individual for control over his or her own body. And it is supported by the idea that sexual pleasure is healthy and can lead to personal fulfillment, as well as to the creation of social bonds that encompass the family—but are not limited to it.

hese revolutionaries worked to create a world in which sex could be enjoyed without fear. Even under today's circumstances, should we let our fears make us feel more isolated and alone? Now is the time to realize how connected to each other we really are. After all, fear will not change the fact that sex is more than the biological source of life. Sex, even in the Era of Aids, remains one of the ways that we can truly become human.

Bibliography

The Age of Desire: Case Histories of A Radical Psycholanalyst, by Joel Kove Pantheon Books, New York. 1981.

An Analysis of the Human Sexual Response, edited by Ruth and Edward Breche Signet Books, New York, 1966.

Beyond Monogamy: Recent Studies of Sexual Alternatives In Marriage, edited b James R. and Lynn G. Smith. Johns Hopkins University Press, Ba timore and London. 1974

Channels of Desire: Mass Images and the Shaping of American Consciousness, b Stuart and Elizabeth Ewen. McGraw-Hill Company, N.Y., St. Loui San Francisco. 1982.

The Culture of Narcissism: American Life in An Age of Diminishing Expectations, b Christopher Lasch. Warner Books, New York. 1979.

De Sade: Selected Writings. Lancer Books, New York. 1953.

Eros & Civilization: A Philosophical Inquiry Into Freud, by Herbert Marcus Vintage Books, New York. 1955.

Gender Advertisements, by Erving Hoffman. Harper Colophon Books, Ne York and London. 1976.

A General Introduction To Psychoanalysis, by Sigmund Freud. Washingto Square Press, New York. 1967.

The Hoax of Romance, by Jo Loudin. Prentice-Hall, Inc., Englewood Cliff N.J. 1981.

Human Sexual Relations: Toward A Redefinition of Sexual Politics, edited by Mik Brake. Pantheon Books, New York. 1982.

The Irresistible Impulse: An Evocative Study of Erotic Notions and Practices Throug the Ages, by Norman Gelb. Paddington Press Ltd., New York an London. 1979.

Love Locked Out, by James Cleugh. Spring Books, London, New York, an Sidney. 1970.

Love In The Western World, by Denis de Rougement. Harper Torchbooks, Ne York, San Francisco, and London, 1974.

Love, Sex and Marriage Through the Ages, by Bernard I Murstein. Spring Publishing Co., New York. 1974.

Male and Female: A Study of the Sexes In A Changing World, by Margaret Mea Dell Publishing Co., New York. 1968.

Man & Woman Boy & Girl: The Differentiation and Dimorphism of Gender Identi from Conception to Maturity, by John Money and Anke A. Ehrhardt. Ne American Library, New York. 1972.

Masculine/Feminine: Readings in Sexual Mythology and the Liberation of Women, edited by Betty and Theodore Roszack. Harper Colophon Books, New York and London. 1969.

The Mermaid and the Minotaur: Sexual Arrangements and Human Malaise, by Dorothy Dinnerstein. Harper Colophon Books, New York and London. 1976.

The Nature and Evolution of the Female, by Mary Jane Sherfey. Vintage Books, New York. 1972.

Orgone, Reich & Eros: Wilhelm Reich's Theory of Life Energy, by W. Edward Mann. Touchstone Books, New York. 1973.

The Party of Eros: Radical Social Thought and the Realization of Freedom, by Richard King. Delta Books, New York. 1981.

Pornography: Men Possessing Women, by Andrea Dworkin. Perigee Books, New York. 1981.

The Sadian Woman and the Ideology of Pornography, by Angela Carter. Pantheon Books, New York. 1978.

Sex, Gender and Society, by Ann Oakley. Harper Colophon Books, New York, San Francisco, and London. 1972.

Sex and Temperament in Three Primitive Societies, by Margaret Mead. New American Library, New York. 1962.

Sexual Behavior and Personal Characteristics, edited by Manfred De Martino. Grove Press, New York. 1966.

Sexual Politics, by Kate Millet. Avon Books, New York. 1970.

Sexual Variance in Society and History, by Vern L. Bullough. University of Chicago Press, Chicago and London. 1976.

Sexuality and the Psychology of Love, by Sigmund Freud. Collier Books, New York. 1963.

Sin, Sickness, and Sanity: A History of Sexual Attitudes, by Vern and Bonnie Bullough. New American Library, New York, 1977.

Sociobiology and Behavior, by David P. Barash. Elsevier Scientific Publishing Company, New York. 1977.

Sociobiology Examined, by Ashley Montagu. Oxford University Press, Oxford, New York, Toronto, and Melbourne. 1980.

A Susan Sontag Reader, by Susan Sontag. Vintage Books, New York. 1982.

Woman in Sexist Society: Studies in Power and Powerlessness, edited by Vivian Gornick and Barbara K. Moran. New American Library, New York. 1971.

The Woman That Never Evolved, by Sarah Blaffer Hrdy, Harvard University Press, Cambridge, Massachusetts, and London, England. 1983.

COMPUTERS
FOR BEGINNERS

ERROL SELKIRK

ILLUSTRATED BY BENNY KANDLER

7 80049 250376

Writing and Reading

ILLUSTRATED BY NAOMI ROSENBLATT

● JUDITH BLACKSTONE & ZORAN JOSIPOVIC

ZEN FOR BEGINNERS

Writing and Reading